Teachi
Prima

*Teaching Foreign Languages in the Primary School* is for every teacher – whether generalist or specialist, trainee or experienced – wanting to confidently introduce foreign language teaching into their classroom.

Based on the author's extensive experience of teaching across Key Stages 1–2, this book provides practical strategies that can be easily implemented in your setting. Offering comprehensive guidance on the pedagogy that underpins language teaching, it covers everything you'll need to teach foreign languages effectively:

- planning, teaching and assessment;
- pedagogical approaches;
- integrating primary languages across the curriculum;
- where to find and how to use good resources;
- using teaching assistants effectively to support language learning;
- inclusive practice;
- using information and communications technology (ICT) in language teaching;
- how to promote children's intercultural understanding.

Illustrated with useful lesson ideas and a range of examples from the classroom, *Teaching Foreign Languages in the Primary School* is an indispensable source of support for all student and practising primary school teachers.

**Sally Maynard** is Senior Lecturer at the Faculty of Education and Theology, York St John University, UK.

# Teaching Foreign Languages in the Primary School

Sally Maynard

Routledge
Taylor & Francis Group

LONDON AND NEW YORK

First published 2012
by Routledge
2 Park Square, Milton Park, Abingdon, Oxon OX14 4RN

Simultaneously published in the USA and Canada
by Routledge
711 Third Avenue, New York, NY 10017

*Routledge is an imprint of the Taylor & Francis Group, an informa business*

*British Library Cataloguing in Publication Data*
A catalogue record for this book is available from the British Library

*Library of Congress Cataloging in Publication Data*
Maynard, Sally.
  Teaching foreign languages in the primary school/Sally Maynard.
  p. cm.
  Includes bibliographical references.
  1. Languages, modern – Study and teaching (Elementary) – Great Britain.
  I. Title.
  LB1578M36 2012
  372.65'0440941 – dc22                                   2011008101

ISBN: 978–0–415–55741–2 (hbk)
ISBN: 978–0–415–55742–9 (pbk)
ISBN: 978–0–203–80502–2 (ebk)

Typeset in Galliard and Gill Sans
by Florence Production Ltd, Stoodleigh, Devon

Printed and bound in Great Britain by
TJ International Ltd, Padstow, Cornwall

# Contents

# Figures

# Preface

The DfES National Languages Strategy, entitled *Languages for All: Languages for Life*, was published on 18 December 2002. Its recommendation for all children in KS2 to have the opportunity of learning a foreign language helped to ensure that all primary schools would regard language learning differently and begin serious implementation. This recommendation is known as the Entitlement. Sir Jim Rose accepted Lord Dearing's recommendation, in the Languages Review published in 2007, that languages be made compulsory in the Curriculum Review, and it seemed that, at last, languages were receiving the attention they deserved.

However, at the time of writing, the future of Primary Languages is again uncertain. With the word 'compulsory' being taken off the agenda, some schools – particularly those with the least confidence or expertise – may retreat, and disregard the Entitlement. Sir Jim Rose's New Primary Curriculum was rejected by the Coalition government and a new review is awaited, with 'a full public consultation of the final drafts of the Programmes of Study early in 2012' (Department for Education July 2011). The White Paper The Importance of Teaching, published in November 2010, recognised language learning as part of the essential knowledge and understanding that all children must have, and secondary-level languages were emphasised as being an important part of the government's education programme.

However, the National Centre for Languages' response, whilst welcoming the emphasis given to languages at secondary level, was as follows:

> If we are to be judged by international standards we must give due importance to languages in the *primary phase*. Over the past decade we have made enormous progress in bringing provision in English primary schools in line with international practice. Over 92% of our primary schools now teach a language and we want to see this taught with the same rigour and challenge as other subjects, across the four years of Key Stage 2. We need to maintain and build on this momentum, through continued support for teachers and schools, so that children in English primary schools enjoy the same benefits from language learning as their peers in high performing countries.
>
> (DfES, 2002)

The United Kingdom lags considerably behind its international peers. In Europe learning languages is compulsory mostly from the ages of seven or eight, and at secondary level up to 16 and sometimes up to 18. A coherent policy of compulsory language learning from primary level needs to be urgently addressed so that the impetus gained since 2002 can be sustained and built upon in order for children not to be disadvantaged and for them to compete in the global workplace.

This book looks at teaching Primary Languages from different perspectives – pedagogy, planning, assessment, using a cross-curricular and embedded approach, intercultural understanding, and developing competence for teachers and trainees. It considers different schools' approaches to teaching languages and assesses the impact that teaching languages in primary schools can make.

Teaching and learning languages at primary level provokes many different reactions: enthusiasm, apathy, controversy, fear, questioning – to name just a few – but it is hoped that, through reading this book, trainees and teachers will understand the relevance and importance of languages in the curriculum, will gain confidence and will be inspired to teach languages.

# Abbreviations

| | |
|---|---|
| AfL | Assessment for learning |
| CILT | National Centre for Languages |
| CLIL | Content Language Integrated Learning |
| CPD | Continuing Professional Development |
| CRF | Common Reference Framework |
| DVD | Digital video disc |
| EAL | English as an additional language |
| EYFS | Early Years Foundation Stage |
| FIFA | Fédération Internationale de Football Association |
| GCSE | General Certificate of Secondary Education |
| HEFCE | Higher Education and Funding Council for England |
| HLTA | Higher level teaching assistant |
| ICT | Information and communications technology |
| ITE | Initial teacher education |
| IWB | Interactive whiteboard |
| KS2 | Key Stage 2 |
| LKS2 | Lower Key Stage 2 |
| MFL | Modern foreign language |
| NALDIC | National Association for Language Development in the Curriculum |
| NC | National Curriculum |
| NQF | National Qualifications Framework |
| Ofsted | Office for Standards in Education |
| PPA | Planning, Preparation and Assessment |
| PSHCE | Personal, Social, Health and Citizenship Education |
| QCDA | Qualifications and Curriculum Development Agency |
| SEN | Special Educational Needs |
| TDA | Teacher Development Agency |
| UKS2 | Upper Key Stage 2 |

# Chapter 1

# Why should languages be introduced at primary level?

This chapter considers:

- a brief history of Primary Languages since the 1970s;
- a discussion of different perspectives as to why languages should be introduced at primary level;
- a picture of national provision and the implementation of Entitlement (see the Preface for a definition of Entitlement);
- teachers' attitudes towards Primary Languages;
- a discussion as to whether Primary Languages should be introduced at KS1 or KS2;
- whether Primary Languages should be aligned with Foundation subjects (History, Geography, Art, Design and Technology, PSHCE) and Humanities subjects (History, R.E. Philosophy, Literature, Languages, Music, Performing Arts), or whether it should be considered as a 'core' subject.

> For too long we have failed to value language skills or recognise the contribution they make to society, to the economy and to raising standards in schools. This has led to a cycle of national underperformance in languages, a shortage of language teachers, low take-up of languages beyond schooling and a workforce unable to meet the demands of a globalised economy.
>
> (DfES, 2002)

This statement from *Languages for All: Languages for Life* is significant because it recognises the fact that our (some would say) dismal achievements in language learning stem from a mind-set rather than an innate inability of UK English-speaking citizens to be successful in learning other languages – an attitude that is widely held. Other views are, of course, that 'everyone speaks English', or 'everyone wants to learn English', or 'English is the language of business'. Paradoxically, it is true to say that people who speak one or two languages other than English are generally held in high esteem and admired. Why, then, should this not translate successfully into classroom performance and attitude?

The overwhelming sentiment seems to be: 'I couldn't do that', or 'I'm no good at languages', or latterly more frequently, 'I don't do languages'. It is crucial not only that our children do learn languages from an early age but that this negative approach be changed. Perhaps the only way this can come about is for trainees and teachers to understand and appreciate how important languages are as part of the curriculum and how they can enhance learning at many levels. Research into the impact of language learning on speaking and listening skills and on children's developing phonological awareness is key. In addition, trainees and teachers need to have opportunities to experience the value of language learning at first hand. It is particularly important for trainees to enter the profession enthused and aware that languages should be an integral part of the curriculum. Trainees' and teachers' attitudes tend to change dramatically once they have participated in some form of overseas placement, whether it is a four-week teaching placement or a two-week assistant-type placement; they come back enthused, committed to teaching languages and with an understanding of how it enhances learning. Not least, they experience the satisfaction of being able to communicate effectively with someone from another country and culture.

Children are motivated **to** learn languages from an early age – there is no doubt about that. Motivation **for** teaching children languages is, however, a different matter. Teaching a foreign language (i.e. a language that is not widely used within the community) at primary level has for years been resisted by many schools and teachers. That is not to say that there have not been schools that have been enthusiastic. Indeed, the current status of Primary Languages is largely owed to a small number of schools and teachers who have remained steadfast in their belief that the primary age is the most appropriate age at which to begin learning a foreign language.

In fairness, much of the indifference was and is connected to a lack of confidence in being able to deliver an effective curriculum in a foreign language. Many primary teachers feel that they just do not have the expertise to teach a foreign language to children when they don't possess the appropriate knowledge or the appropriate qualifications. In addition, their own language-learning experiences may have been negative and they simply do not feel inspired or interested to teach the subject. The crowded curriculum is another factor in schools' reluctance to develop language teaching. However, with the huge amount of support and resources that is now available this is really no longer a valid objection. Government support is evident within the KS2 Framework for Languages, the National Centre for Languages (CILT) national training for all KS2 teachers, the CILT Primary Languages website, the Qualifications and Curriculum Development Agency's (QCDA) schemes of work for KS2 languages, the Upskilling Specification (a CILT resource aimed at developing teachers' linguistic competence) and from any number of commercial and online resources that have exploded onto the market since the 2009/2010 Entitlement was announced.

The model adopted by head teachers in all the schools in which I worked was for me, as a specialist, to teach all the classes in both Key Stages, whilst in the early days my own class was covered by another teacher and latterly by teaching assistants during planning, preparation and assessment (PPA) time. PPA time usually constitutes 10 per cent of the working week – generally part of a morning or an afternoon. The former was positively received, on the whole, by the class teachers because a) they didn't have to do the teaching and b) they could view the lessons as part of their professional development.

From my perspective, however, although the children thoroughly enjoyed the lessons and were extremely motivated, there was hardly any follow-up and many lessons were spent revisiting and reviewing previous work, which meant that the children made slower progress. In addition, because my lessons were 'extra' and were, for the most part, comprised of games and songs, children viewed the lessons not as an integral part of the curriculum but more as a fun 'brain-break'. Often the lessons interrupted something else because of the nature of the school's (and my) timetable, which didn't help if children were in the middle of, say, creative writing. The teachers, understandably, were less keen on this aspect of the language teaching because children invariably finished my input on a 'high' and were not so keen to carry on with 'proper work' – as I vividly remember one teacher commenting. This is not to say that language learning was unsuccessful using this model: on the contrary, it was received very positively by children, staff, parents and governors alike, and was widely recognised as enriching and enhancing the children's learning overall.

Schools have adopted different approaches to teaching languages; for example, languages clubs have been popular, but this approach tends to be elitist and denies the right of all children to have the opportunity to learn another language. The 'add-on' or 'extra' approach has engendered a perspective amongst children and staff that learning foreign languages is not a serious subject because (a) they are not learned from the outset of a child's school career and (b) they have traditionally been taught at secondary level, when some feel that children are more efficient learners.

As a language specialist, I concurred with the view of many teachers (particularly secondary) that languages are an area of the curriculum that necessitate specialist teaching, that they are not a subject that can be 'genned up' on before each lesson or one in which the teacher is 'one step ahead'. However, in recent years I have come to change that view and feel that class teachers, provided they have the appropriate resources and support, are best placed to teach languages at primary level. This view will be expanded upon later.

In order to comprehend the current status of Primary Languages, it will be helpful to look briefly at the journey the subject has taken to reach this point.

## History of Primary Languages provision from 1964 to the present – an overview

In 1964 a pilot scheme was introduced in selected schools in England and Wales to teach French from September of that year to 8-year-olds and then to extend the scheme to a further year group the following year until all pupils in the 8–11 age range were involved. The cohort selection criterion for inclusion was based purely on birth date, and was thus 'characterized by a wide range of ability'. The Burstall report (1974), which evaluated the project, seemed to indicate this as a negative aspect. It is unlikely that differentiation occurred within the teaching and, as such, this perhaps further negated findings.

The purpose of the pilot project was to determine whether it was feasible to extend the teaching of foreign languages to pupils in the primary phase of schooling. French was the only viable language, as the available expertise in other European languages was much less. The scheme was to be delivered by teachers who had received in-service training, and not by specialist French-language teachers. Burstall *et al.*'s report states that 'arrangements were made to provide continuity of teaching at the secondary stage, so that all pupils taking part in the experiment would be able to continue learning French without interruption for at least 5 years'.

The scheme was beset with a number of problems from the outset – staffing issues and the lack of training during the first term of the project resulted in the first year being more exploratory than anything else and threw up questions as to the authority of the results gathered from the first cohort. As a result of these problems, pupils did not receive an introduction to French that could be compared to a usual beginning at secondary level. A third cohort (instead of the originally envisaged two cohorts) was studied from September 1968 to further validate findings and to, hopefully, draw positive conclusions about the feasibility of introducing French at primary level. However, the cohorts could not be reasonably compared because they were under study for different periods of time. Nevertheless, the aims of the study were as follows:

- to investigate the long-term development of pupils' attitudes towards foreign language learning;
- to discover whether pupils' levels of achievement in French were related to their attitudes;
- to examine the effect of certain pupil variables (e.g. age, gender, socio-economic status, perception of parental encouragement, employment expectations);
- to investigate whether teachers' attitudes and expectations significantly affected the attitudes and achievements of pupils;
- to examine whether the early introduction of French had a significant impact on achievement in other areas of the curriculum.

Burstall *et al.*'s report concluded overall that there was no significant improvement in children's attainment at secondary level, and the damning findings of the Burstall report echoed resoundingly through primary schools for a number of years.

There were, however, pockets of resistance to the findings during the 1980s and 1990s, and gradually the possibility of languages being taught at primary level began to surface again and gathered momentum. Schools were very often working in isolation or in small clusters. Some authorities, notably Kent, worked hard to raise the profile and engender enthusiasm. The pilot schemes in Scotland did (and still do) marvellous work.

*Languages: The Next Generation* (Nuffield 2000) and the subsequent *Languages for All: Languages for Life* (DfES 2002) are the significant reports that have started the UK on the way to achieving targets for language learning from primary level. From September 2010 all primary schools had to deliver an 'Entitlement' to all children in KS2 so that they might have the opportunity to learn a language other than English. A longitudinal study published in 2009 gave the figure of 18 per cent of schools that were likely not to be ready to provide this Entitlement. Although this figure was relatively high, it should be noted that resources and support were and are available to all schools to help them implement the Entitlement requirements.

So, one argument for languages to be taught a primary level is to familiarise children with language learning strategies (LLS) from an early age, both in order for those strategies to be developed and also to enable children to easily transfer these skills at secondary level to further their language learning and perhaps also learn other languages. We need to take away the 'can't do' mentality and change it to 'can do' (and to do it well). This can then, hopefully, impact on the *Languages for All* conclusions in that performance levels can be raised, more children will take up language learning at GCSE and beyond and the workforce will be better equipped for the global economy. As long ago as 1995 the *Guardian* stated: 'evidence indicates that linguists experience less unemployment than many other graduates'. This suggests not that languages are an extra, but rather that they are vital to children in improving their job prospects. In a 2008 report on graduates and their early careers, the Higher Education and Funding Council for England (HEFCE) stated: 'Of the strategically important subjects, engineering had the highest mean salary for employed graduates after six months. When considering employment three and a half years after graduating, modern foreign language graduates have the highest mean salary.' The HEFCE also noted in 2009, in a report on the health of modern foreign languages at higher education level, that

'In the longer term, the Government's decision to make languages compulsory for all seven year olds from 2011 should help to create more linguistically and culturally aware young people who want to study languages at University' (Worton, 2009). At the time of writing, however, the decision has been made not to proceed with the primary curriculum that would make languages compulsory – but it is important to note that the entitlement stands and languages should have been evident in all primary schools from the academic year 2009–10.

## Psychological and social arguments in favour of an early start to language learning

It is in the early/primary years that basic skills and concepts of literacy are taught. Children are learning and absorbing their mother-tongue language skills in speaking and listening as well as in reading and writing on a daily basis. They are increasing and consolidating their knowledge of the patterns and functions of the mother tongue in a situation which is familiar and comfortable for them. Each year most children are taught by one teacher, with whom they can develop a secure and trusting relationship. The introduction of language learning in this context would seem to have great benefits for the learner and it seems reasonable to suggest, then, that the basic concepts of languages should also be taught within this age range. Learning languages is far from easy, but we know that children all over the world persevere in the task of acquiring their mother tongue and the majority are remarkably successful. The primary classroom affords the opportunity for teachers to embed language teaching (i.e. to encompass and relate to other subjects) and to develop intercultural understanding as well as linguistic skills.

Bruner (1966) stated that 'the importance of early experience is only dimly sensed today'. Whether younger children are faster language learners is unclear, but the layman's view that they are faster at learning languages tends to stem from observations that, under certain conditions, young children do become fluent in a second language when they have been exposed to two different languages from a very early age. These are generally specialised conditions that cannot usually be repeated in a school situation (apart from an immersion approach), but language learning takes time, and from that standpoint alone, the earlier it commences, the better.

Physiological reasons have been mooted that favour an early start to language learning. The Critical Period Hypothesis (CPH) (Lenneberg 1967), which suggests that pupils at the age of puberty experience difficulties in mastering accents, is an interesting one. If indeed there is a 'window of opportunity' of language learning during the period when one acquires the first language, then it would seem sensible to take advantage of this. It is a simplistic notion, however, and the existence of the CPH is fiercely debated. Researchers argue that there are adult and older learners of a second language who acquire good accents, in which case 'other powerful explanations are needed to account for the dramatic decline in ultimate achievement generally seen in later second language learners compared to young children' (Birdsong 1999).

All primary teachers are aware of harnessing children's motivation at primary level – less inhibited primary children will engage readily in conversation and 'have a go', provided they are in a situation where they are not anxious and where they are engaged in giving and receiving purposeful messages. Encouraging and giving all children the opportunity to participate in Primary Languages learning is vital, and the primary classroom is the ideal situation for this to flourish. Krashen (1981) states this succinctly: 'language acquisition, first or second, occurs when comprehension of real messages occurs, and when the acquirer is not "on the defensive"'. Language acquisition is a slow process but the drip, drip approach of children having to use language every day in meaningful circumstances within the primary classroom (e.g. the teacher asking what time it is, or whether the child requires a packed lunch or school dinner) means that children will absorb and develop their listening skills and grammatical understanding without extensive drilling of rules, and it will prepare them to produce words and phrases when they are ready to do so. They will be looking for meaning and will, if encouraged and praised, take every opportunity to practise. Anyone who has lived in another country knows that it takes a while to be able to attempt to speak in that country's language; **listening** and **understanding** come first.

Another argument is that the desire for languages to be taught at primary level will not go away – in the 1990s it was parental pressure that made primary schools introduce languages; indeed in the *Times Educational Supplement* on 24 March 1995 Dorothy Lepkowska wrote: 'The rapid but ad hoc growth of primary language courses – most have been introduced in the past five years, [has been] mainly inspired by parental pressure.' It is not unreasonable to assume that parents still feel the same way.

Examples of positive parental attitudes can be cited from a 1996 seven-year Primary Languages project carried out by the author in a North Yorkshire school of 250 children where, in response to questions relating to when their child should commence foreign language learning, 90 per cent of parents felt that it should be statutory at primary level, with 56 per cent stating that it should commence in Foundation and 30 per cent in KS1. These attitudes were mirrored in subsequent projects in different schools in 1998, 2002 and 2006, the major difference being that evidence suggested that **all** parents in the most recent project felt that language learning should commence at the Foundation stage.

Important areas for parents in the consideration of why Primary Languages should be taught were:

- that learning a language at Primary Level would develop confidence for further study at secondary level;
- the importance of developing the ability to communicate in another language;
- that learning another language would be good for future job prospects;
- the importance of developing an interest in and awareness of other cultures;
- that children enjoyed learning a language at a younger age and were best placed and more motivated to do so.

Parental perspectives do tend to be positive, with most wanting their children to have as varied and as rich an education as possible and one that will contribute to their long-term employment prospects and to their motivation for learning. It is important to note also that no negative feedback to teachers was encountered at all in relation to Primary Languages learning in these schools.

Perspectives vary enormously on whether or not languages should be and can be introduced. Trainees' perspectives tend to be positive. If they possess any competence at all in another language, they are often keen to develop this, and appreciate opportunities to participate in overseas placements or upskilling sessions. They also recognise that having that 'extra string to their bow' makes them more marketable. There is no doubt that the international and global dimensions enrich schools' curricula considerably, provided that someone is willing to take it on.

There are now many teachers who are willing to take on language teaching and recognise the positive impact that it has on children's learning. Since the awareness of Entitlement, and, in particular, when it was thought that languages were going to be made compulsory, there has definitely been a swing towards languages' being encouraged in schools and teachers' beginning to see it as an integral part of primary learning. The development of children's phonological understanding and the link to language learning is starting to be appreciated, and many teachers are relating phonics teaching to foreign-language learning. This is the change in mind-set that many have been working towards and it is very encouraging. The challenge will be to see if this is sustained and whether schools treat it seriously and refrain from scheduling language sessions in time that is allocated to teachers for PPA. All primary teachers are now entitled to the allocation of 10 per cent of their working week to plan, prepare and assess work and lessons. When teachers are out of their classroom during this time, there has been a tendency to allocate other staff (often teaching assistants) to teach subjects that teachers perhaps feel less confident in, lack interest in or even deem less important – and this can include languages. Religious Education is often another casualty of this attitude.

If physiological, psychological and social views are accepted, it seems that the optimum age at which to teach another language should be as early as possible, that is to say, at the Foundation stage or even at Nursery stage. Learning a language from the outset of a pupil's school career should lead to acceptance of and respect for the subject as an integral part of the curriculum and will not engender the attitude that, because the subject is started later, it is not as important. This does not necessarily mean that young children are better learners than adolescents or adults, but it does mean that, given the right conditions, they can improve and develop quickly, acquiring a good basic knowledge of a second language.

There is some contention as to where languages should 'sit' within the curriculum. The independent review of the Primary Curriculum put them, quite rightly, with understanding English, communication and languages. This indicates that the subject should be practised on a regular basis, not treated as an add-on or covered at the end of a half term to show that it has been 'done'. If languages are aligned with Foundation subjects, a rigorous approach is less likely to flourish because different Foundation subjects are covered in different terms and not throughout the year. Schools will need guidance and have to undergo inspection on the implementation of Primary Languages on a regular basis, as with all subject areas, in order to sustain confidence and competence.

Whether Primary Languages continues to thrive and take its rightful place in the primary curriculum will depend on future government policy and funding. As previously mentioned, the enthusiasm for teaching languages will not recede, as most schools that have made a strong commitment to implementing languages will continue to do so; such schools see benefits far beyond the learning of a foreign language. It is essential that there is a coherent policy of teaching languages in the primary sector of schooling, in order that transition issues are addressed successfully and progressively. The CILT's 2010 'Primary Languages Survey' (CILT 2010) noted that 83 per cent of local authorities wished to see Primary Languages made a compulsory part of the curriculum. In addition, the CILT stated that 'advisers also stressed the need for continuity and coherence from primary to secondary and the need for a learning continuum in languages through to secondary school'. These issues are vital in ensuring that our children are able to build upon and achieve in language learning.

The European Commission (2008) states: 'The more languages you know, the more of a person you are.' It is necessary for government and schools to take this on board so as to help produce the rounded individuals we all want to see as part of society.

## Reflection

- What are my own views on teaching languages in the primary classroom and what has influenced my views? To what extent do my own language-learning experiences help or hinder my attitudes?
- How can teaching assistants be best used to support the delivery of Primary Languages?
- How can I develop my confidence, understanding and practice of teaching languages?
- How would I respond to an assertion by a colleague that younger children may confuse phonemes in the mother tongue and a second language?
- If asked to do so by my head teacher, how would I enthuse staff to teach Primary Languages in a school where negative attitudes prevail?

# Chapter 2

# Pedagogical approaches to teaching Primary Languages

This chapter considers:

- how to make Primary Languages relevant in the curriculum;
- choice and use of resources;
- the delivery of languages in the primary classroom;
- how to consolidate primary language learning – revisit/review/teach/practise/apply;
- teaching in the target language;
- good questioning to promote effective learning.

## Making Primary Languages relevant

Children learn best when they are learning or doing a task for a purpose. Everyone learns best if they understand why they are learning and what the ultimate aim is.

It is probably true to say that this is one of the principal reasons for our nation's dismal failure in language learning. Too many lessons have concentrated in the past on irrelevant context and content. In addition, it is hard to convince children (and adults) that learning another language is important when, as previously mentioned, everyone seems able to speak English, when it is the language of choice for business and culture, and also when everyone appears to want to speak English. But 'English is not enough. Young people from the UK are at a growing disadvantage in the recruitment market', 'the UK desperately needs more language teachers'. These are further quotes from the Nuffield Foundation's inquiry (Nuffield Foundation 2000).

Traditionally, children have started learning a new language at secondary level, in Year 7. To be confronted with acquiring all four skills at once – reading, writing, speaking and listening – is daunting in the extreme. Small wonder that many children have been 'turned off' learning languages because it is 'too hard'! If children are allowed to reflect on how they learned their own language, they will realise that for many years they were exposed to it aurally and orally before there was any kind of serious attempt to read and write. Learning a second language should be treated with the same approach, as far as possible.

Being able to communicate with someone from another country in their native tongue is a joy and gives a real sense of achievement. We all know people who can speak several languages, and these people are universally admired. Why, then, has it been so difficult to transfer the desire to achieve this into the classroom? One reason could be that children do not envisage themselves in situations where they may have to communicate in another language; their expectations are low.

The primary practitioner can emphasise the global nature of society in the classroom in order to help children understand that they may meet people both now and in the future who speak other languages, and also perhaps to help them aspire to travel and interact with children and people of other countries and cultures. This can be achieved, for example, through partner schools and by schools' taking advantage of the many schemes that are available for hosting students and teachers from other countries. The global dimension of education should be highlighted so as to enable children to see that speaking another language is both relevant and beneficial. This aspect will be further developed in Chapter 6.

How else can children be helped to see the relevance of language learning? Many schools are starting to take children on trips to other countries, usually in Year 5 or 6, when they can obviously try out their developing linguistic skills at first hand. If a school takes on the commitment to such trips in its school calendar and long-term planning, children will look forward to and anticipate them with excitement. They will realise that at some point in the future they will be talking to children (perhaps from a partner school) in the language that the school is teaching. It cannot be emphasised enough how beneficial such trips are, not just for children's language-learning skills, but also for many other areas of the curriculum. The history of the area visited can be looked at, as well as geographical features, religious festivals and art – all contributing as well to children's intercultural understanding. Trips abroad will open up a whole new dimension to the children, which can only benefit them in later life. What better way to develop intercultural understanding than to immerse the children in different cultures from an early age? This aspect is also developed further in Chapter 6.

Primary methodology is wholly appropriate for language learning and the linguistic form of intelligence because, for the most part, it should concentrate initially on speaking and listening skills. Language learning enhances these skills and cross-curricular benefits will be observed as the traditional boundaries between arts and science are broken down to allow problem solving and thinking to be at the heart of learning development. The emphasis should be on language use and children should be taught to communicate, alongside language-learning strategies such as repetition and rhyme. If the relevance of language learning is not clear, then it is unlikely that motivation and interest will be sustained into later learning. By the time children reach Year 7, they should be able to communicate reasonably effectively in the target language and their knowledge can be built on to achieve good proficiency by the end of KS3. It is hoped that if children gain confidence in language learning, more will take up GSCE options in languages at KS4. Schools should aspire to this in order to address the grim situation that our language teaching at secondary level and beyond now faces.

Learning a language in the earlier years eliminates, to a large extent, the tedium and inappropriate vocabulary (such as colours, numbers) that are below the cognitive development and understanding of secondary-age children. The choice of resources and the content of any Primary Language programme should be carefully decided on and evaluated at every stage and within each year group and class, so that both children's interest can be sustained and linguistic and cognitive development can be achieved. Transition issues also need to be addressed, and these are explored in depth in Chapter 7.

## Choice and use of resources

The KS2 Framework for Languages provides for schools what its title implies – a coherent framework to work from so that schools can ensure that they cover the essential aspects of language learning that are appropriate for KS2. The Framework also enables and assists schools in ensuring that children progress appropriately across the Key Stage. It is available to download from CILT's Primary Languages website, www.primarylanguages.org.uk, along with a vast amount of support of various kinds. These consist of many DVD examples of teaching showing embedding (e.g. within daily routine or cross-curricular links), active learning (e.g. drama, puppets and story-telling), inclusion, ICT, celebrating languages (e.g. assemblies and special events), using community languages, progression and continuity as well as advice on planning, assessment, resources, the international dimension and using the KS2 Framework. The DVD clips can be downloaded, as well as transcript files, audio files and continuing professional development (CPD) information. The site is being continuously updated and developed and is an invaluable resource for teachers and trainees.

Many choices of resource are now available to schools that take into account different types of learner and teacher. Most are aimed at non-specialists, but they vary enormously. Schools need to think carefully about the appropriate resource before committing to any scheme. The CILT Primary Languages website offers advice as to what aspects should be considered.

Primary Languages is no different from any other subject, in that just using a scheme is not enough. Teachers and trainees need to be allowed to use their creativity and imagination to develop topics. This is the reason for most people's choice to work in primary, and it should not be dulled. Help and support are essential, but so are inventiveness and inspiration. If children see that teachers are using originality and flair, they too will be inspired and motivated.

In addition to the many published resources, the Qualifications and Curriculum Development Agency's (QCDA) schemes of work for French, German and Spanish were sent to all schools and are excellent guidelines. They can be downloaded from the CILT website: www.primarylanguages.org.uk/resources/qcda_schemes_of_work.aspx.

Also available are the Teacher Development Agency (TDA) versions of the QCDA schemes of work, which have been adapted by CILT to further support initial teacher training. These are available to download in French, German and Spanish: www.primarylanguages.org.uk/resources/schemes_of_work/tda_schemes_of_work.aspx.

There is also a Portuguese scheme of work, which has been developed by Lambeth Council and is available to download: www.primarylanguages.org.uk/resources/schemes_of_work/portuguese_schemes_of_work.aspx.

## Delivery

Schools will have different models for the delivery of Primary Languages, depending, for example, on expertise and on school policy in relation to the time allocated for the subject.
Examples of models might be:

- An external specialist primary-trained teacher; there is likely to be one session a week for each year group, which will consist of discrete teaching. Lessons may or may not be followed up by class teachers.
- An internal specialist teacher or teaching assistant who may deliver sessions during the class teacher's PPA time, for example; still probably one session a week. Again, lessons may or may not be followed up by the class teacher.

- A native speaker who is not a trained primary teacher but who delivers conversational lessons with the class teacher present. The number of sessions is not likely to be more than two per week, and will probably be one. Again, lessons may or may not be followed up by the class teacher.
- A secondary language teacher who may be part of a cluster scheme and who may teach in all feeder schools. Again, sessions are likely to be one a week and may or may not be followed up by the class teacher.
- The class teacher, who delivers one or more discrete sessions and then follows up work in other subject areas throughout the week.

Clearly, the class teacher has the most opportunity to follow up learning and this is the desirable model. The one-session-a-week model also has potential to be followed up, but this rests completely with the school's policy and the willingness or otherwise of class teachers to do so. I have witnessed all the above models in different schools, implemented with varying degrees of success. The most successful schools regard it as essential that the languages policy should be a whole-school policy, regardless of the available expertise, in order for children to receive consistency.

Discrete sessions are successful when they follow a format similar to phonics teaching, i.e. revisit/review, teach, practise and apply. (This is expanded below.) It is helpful to plan sessions in this way, with opportunities to state objectives, name resources, specify target language and evaluate sessions. Figure 2.1 is an example of a weekly Primary Languages pro forma that takes these aspects into account. Figure 2.2 is an individual session pro forma that offers opportunities for further reflection and evaluation.

## Revisit/review

When children are receiving only one session per week (and perhaps no follow-up within class), revisit/review is enormously important. Children need to have plenty of opportunity for consolidation and to practise what they have learned previously. For the class teacher, revisit/review is not just for discrete sessions but for any vocabulary that is being revisited during embedded sessions as well. For assessment purposes it is essential that all children have an opportunity to participate and that their responses and contributions are monitored as far as possible in terms of pronunciation, intonation, accuracy and comprehension. Children's phonics knowledge will assist them in understanding and attempting different pronunciations in the target language and revisit/review offers excellent opportunities to increase and reinforce their knowledge about language. Children will recognise cognates and similar phonemes, but at the same time will deepen their phonological awareness through listening to and producing different sounds.

## Teach and practise

Any new vocabulary or objective will be included here and give primary practitioners the opportunity to do what they know best and are familiar with. Games, songs, drama, story-telling, PE activities, art and design activities, quizzes, surveys and adaptations of maths activities work perfectly well alongside tried and tested language-teaching strategies such as flashcards, repetition, songs and rhymes which can be used with a primary 'touch'. Many examples of teaching strategies are given in Chapters 3, 4 and 6.

| Primary Languages weekly plan | | | Date | | | | |
|---|---|---|---|---|---|---|---|
| Day | KS2 Framework objectives | Links to PNS/literacy | Discrete or embedded session – if embedded specify which subject area | Revisit/review | Teach | Practise | Apply |
| M | | | | | | | |
| T | | | | | | | |
| W | | | | | | | |
| T | | | | | | | |
| F | | | | | | | |
| Resources | | | | Target Language | | | |
| Evaluation | | | | | | | |

Figure 2.1  Primary Languages weekly plan pro forma

| YEAR GROUP: 6 | NO. OF CHILDREN: 25 | ORGANISATION OF CHILDREN: Whole class, then working in pairs | | |
|---|---|---|---|---|

**SUBJECT/AREA OF LEARNING** (KS2 FRAMEWORK FOR LANGUAGES) ATTAINMENT TARGETS FOR LANGUAGES)

| | | | DATE: | SESSION BEGINS:<br>SESSION ENDS: |
|---|---|---|---|---|

O6.3: understand longer and more complex phrases or sentences
O6.4: use spoken language confidently
IU 6.3: Present information about an aspect of culture
NC 1.1 a-b, 1.2 a-c, 1.3 a-b

**LEARNING OBJECTIVE(S):**
To recognise, describe and imitate the painting style of the Impressionists
To be able to describe painting and explain preferences with justification
To recognise colours effectively – particularly dark and light

**SUCCESS CRITERIA (DIFFERENTIATED AS APPROPRIATE):**
I can name the features of the Impressionists' paintings in French
I can describe a picture in French
I can name different colours
I can paint a picture in the style of the Impressionists

**ASSESSMENT PLANS:**

| WHO | WHAT | HOW | WHEN | WHO |
|---|---|---|---|---|
| Whole class | Language competence<br>Painting competence | Through targeted questioning and observations of paintings | Throughout session | Class Teacher |

**LEARNING OBJECTIVE** (in child friendly terms)

**PRIOR LEARNING TO BE REVIEWED**
Colours in French
Instructions for painting

**WHAT RESOURCES DO I NEED TO PREPARE/COLLECT BEFORE THE LESSON?**
Paper
Paint
Palettes
Water containers
Different size brushes
Sketching pencils

**CONTEXT OF THE LANGUAGE**
Content language integrated learning in study of Impressionists

**ORGANISATION OF OTHER ADULTS**
n/a

**USE OF ICT** (if appropriate)
Presentation of picture on IWB

**CROSS-CURRICULAR LINKS**
NC Art & Design 3a, 4a and c

**SPECIAL CONSIDERATIONS, INCLUDING HEALTH AND SAFETY, BEHAVIOURAL ISSUES, TIMETABLE ISSUES, ETC.**
Tyler – easily distracted. Not to sit with Aiden
Paints need to be cleared away promptly at 10.20 as assembly is at 10.30

**Target language script (teacher)**
Vous voyez ….
Que remarquez-vous?
Faites d'abord …
Une esquisse/un dessin
Les coups de pinceau/les couleurs brisées

**Target language (pupil)**
Je peux dessiner d'abord?
Je ne comprends pas …
J'utilise quelle brosse ?
Comment on fait des coups de pinceau?

| | Time | Children's activities to meet learning objectives (differentiated where appropriate) | Resources |
|---|---|---|---|
| Introduction/context | 5 mins | Les couleurs – révision<br>Demandez aux enfants s'ils connaissent l'artiste<br>Qu'est-ce qu'ils savent au sujet des impressionnistes?<br>Décrivez les couleurs | |
| Main teaching input/activities | 10 mins | Qu'est-ce que vous voyez?<br>Vous voyez quelles couleurs?<br>On va peindre! | |
| Plenary | 10 mins | Qu'est-ce que vous avez trouvé difficile?<br>Regardez cette image …<br>Qu'est-ce que vous remarquez? | |

**EVALUATION OF LEARNING:**
What was the impact of your teaching on the children's learning?

**EVALUATION OF TEACHING:**
What went well and why?

What could have been improved and how?

Figure 2.2 Primary Languages discrete session plan

When the objective has been introduced, children will need plenty of opportunity to practise, with the teacher as facilitator. Asking whole-class questions, then groups, and then asking for individual responses gives children the chance to listen several times and to develop confidence before attempting to answer individually.

Children need to be challenged so as to ensure progression and sustain motivation. It is particularly important that children are allowed to make mistakes, in order to enable reflection and facilitate structuring of their own sentences and phrases. There are very complex mechanisms at work here, relating to mother-tongue syntax and the application of the syntax of the 'new' language.

For practising it is essential to:

- ensure adequate listening time;
- ensure adequate practising time – give children time to 'think' before they respond to questions and avoid 'putting them on the spot';
- plan for all children to be engaged;
- assess confidence – have the children 'got it'?;
- ensure variation – e.g. different games, songs, resources, perhaps writing activities, flashcards, cue cards, role play;
- use the target language wherever possible.

## Application

An activity that requires children to work in twos and threes or small groups moves them on to the next stage of independent thought and communication.

An example of a discrete session is given in Figure 2.2.

The CILT website sums up the approach to application:

When children are ready to deepen their understanding, activities to consolidate need to:

- Provide plenty of opportunity to be creative with the new language
- Enable children to practise language often
- Enable children to communicate: i.e. understand and be understood
- Enable memorising
- Apply prior knowledge
- Provide opportunities for the teacher to model writing and role play
- Enable children to use dictionaries when appropriate.

## Display

Using display in language teaching is helpful for children in learning languages, just as in any other area of the primary curriculum. For example, having instructions and often-used phrases permanently on display helps children to assimilate the grapheme–phoneme correspondence in the target language because they can be referred to during sessions. Or perhaps, if you are studying a particular artist, have examples of their work on display in order to be able to refer to them during sessions in which you are embedding the target language. Displays can be presented in both English and the target language – particularly if a topic in the language is being taught in a cross-curricular approach. Examples of this might be a picture of a human figure, or a Spanish song if children are studying the Tudors and the Spanish Armada. An excellent website, www.newseum.org, allows you to see the headlines in different newspapers from around the world, which would link well to literacy objectives in teaching about headings and sub-headings; pages could be printed off, or the website could be displayed on the IWB to enable the children to research. The possibilities are endless. A well-thought-out display is a tool to engage and stimulate children, and all children benefit from seeing their own work valued and put on show.

Visits to other countries should be celebrated and children's adventures can be presented to the whole school.

Displays involving community languages are helpful to create an inclusive atmosphere in the classroom. 'Welcome' displays in the school entrance that display all the languages spoken in the school are becoming increasingly common. Welcome displays in the schools' target language are also widely used; they give status to the language and give positive messages to both children and visitors.

## Teaching in the target language

Teaching in the target language is fine if you have a good grasp of the language, but not so easy if you don't. Many courses and resources talk about using the target language and encourage teachers to do so. Use of the target language should be meaningful and purposeful for both teachers and children, so that progress can be made. If possible, any communication that would be a normal part of a lesson (e.g. 'Can I sharpen my pencil?' 'It's hot: can I open a window?') should be considered and attempted. This is all very well and laudable, but the reality is that those who can't very often don't – and understandably so. Some questions that can be considered here in relation to using the target language are:

- Is it better if you do?
- Does it matter if you don't?
- What if you can't?

### Is it better if you do?

Clearly, the more the children can be exposed to the target language, the better. I have talked about children listening and assimilating before they can speak, and of course it is of enormous benefit to them if a teacher or native speaker uses the target language effectively and with confidence. However, realistically, the majority of teachers will not be using the target language with any kind of fluency. The CILT has an upskilling specification that Primary Languages co-ordinators and trainers are encouraged to use or to adapt for use in their local authorities; but, as discussed, listening comes before speaking, for the teacher as well as for the pupil. It cannot be realistically expected that the majority of teachers will be using the target language fluently for some time. However, teachers can be encouraged to participate in projects such as the two-week teacher project, which can involve their travelling to the country of their school's target language to develop their competence. They can also use authentic CDs and DVD clips, which will help. While use of the target language is important, its use has to be judged well so that learners are not demoralised if they do not understand what is required of them. It is wholly appropriate to use the mother tongue to clarify meaning when the situation warrants it.

### Does it matter if you don't?

There will be teachers who do not use the target language at all; indeed a teacher I spoke to recently looked puzzled when I asked if she did, and had evidently not given it much thought. She had a good GCSE in French, but speaking in French during her lessons in any kind of instructional sense did not feature, apart from teaching children the vocabulary objectives for that session. I doubt very much that she is alone in this, and I am sure that many teachers take the same approach. The children still enjoyed their lessons, however, and were making progress. So what can be concluded from this? One factor that is important, I feel, is that for these particular children, Year 3, learning the language is new and exciting; but what about when they reach Years 5 and 6? Their expectations are likely to be higher, and they themselves may wish to use the target language more. Will not using the target language matter at that stage, and if it is not used do we risk developing negative attitudes such as those that my trainees sometimes mention? These include indifference to language learning (perhaps as a result of their own poor language learning experiences), a perception that learning a language is too hard, or that learning another language is unnecessary because English is so widely taught in other countries. I think it will impact negatively on children's learning if they do not see the teacher using the language wherever possible.

Not using the target language would probably be regarded by a linguist as very surprising, as to use it is so much a part of any language learning. A teacher who does not have any kind of background in language learning is very likely to resort to the mother tongue as much as possible. They do not know **how** to use the target language, and this is not surprising; many trainees cite to me their secondary language learning as having been completely devoid of any kind of spoken element on the part of their teachers, and I suspect that many teachers have had the same experience. This has implications for training, in that using the target language needs to be modelled to trainees and teachers during training, and their reticence and inhibitions will need to be addressed in order for them to succeed and feel confident.

Scripting in planning what the teacher intends to say might seem laborious, but is extremely effective. This is not to say that teachers should read from a script, but considering and practising the lesson format will significantly aid progress and confidence. Scripting allows a train of thought to reach fruition and identifies weak areas. In addition, predicting and reflecting on the language that pupils will need to know in response to activities will be beneficial for both pupils and teachers. For example, when playing a game, children might need to know:

- It's my turn!
- It's not his/her turn
- What do I do next?
- How many do I need?
- He/she is cheating!

Constructions will vary from the very simple, i.e. 'Yes' or 'No', to the more complex, such as, for example, 'Do I need to do this?'

Looking at the vocabulary and meaning from the children's perspective will aid development in the teacher's use of the target language.

Purposely writing something in error, e.g. misspelling a word, can also be a tool to aid progress in the target language – children may simply call out 'non', but this can evolve into, for example, 'Vous n'avez pas raison!' or 'Ce n'est pas correcte!'

## What if I can't?

Lack of subject knowledge is one of the key areas that teachers and trainees worry about in terms of Primary Languages delivery. Demonstration lessons in which the target language is used with fluency will not allay their fears; reassurance and modelling at different levels to match teachers' and trainees' capabilities and to build confidence are far better.

It is important that children are aware of basic greetings and politeness phrases that are used consistently at the beginning and end of each session. Using these phrases in each session will enable both teacher and pupils to practise regularly. Praise language is also essential. If teachers use anything, it should be these, in order to encourage children in their learning.

It is also helpful for children to know how to communicate lack of understanding, and questions and statements such as 'Does everyone understand' or 'I don't understand' are crucial. **Making mistakes should be part of the atmosphere in the classroom, as children need to know that errors are part of the learning process.**

Just giving one-word imperatives or utterances is a perfectly acceptable starting-point, and levels of understanding can be measured in terms of delivery and response times. For example, in a PE warm-up children will understand perfectly well one-word instructions such as 'Marchez!' 'Courez!' and 'Arrêtez!' given along with miming and gestures to derive and consolidate meaning. (Incidentally, it is important to include the exclamation mark with imperatives – a native French speaker I was talking to recently is regularly enraged that this is forgotten!) As confidence is gained, this can then be developed into two-word utterances, e.g. 'Marchez vite!' The teacher can then move on to semi-fluent questions and commands, e.g. 'Ecoutez! Sautez comme un lapin!' Children will progress perfectly well with this step-by-step approach and teachers will gain confidence the more they use it. This approach will also give the teacher plenty of opportunity to practise and to improve pronunciation. Linguists have bad days, when pronunciation isn't everything it should be, so teachers shouldn't feel intimidated by 'specialists'; we can all improve!

Visual aids can help considerably in teachers' use of the target language, particularly when they are used regularly, as in classroom routines. I have already mentioned referring to displayed classroom instructions such as listen, look, sit down, stand up, etc. (which could include a picture as well as the written form). Creating a list of instructions that are used on a regular basis and considering what will be needed in different situations will help. Satchwell and de Silva's lists in *Speak Up! Getting Talking in the Classroom* are a good starting-point for communication in the classroom and can be easily adapted for individual use.

Figure 2.3 shows a pro forma that trainees are given to monitor, reflect on and assess their use of the target language.

Progression is another issue for teachers – the target language used in Year 3 will be different from that used in Year 6; and the poor Year 6 teacher who has had little experience of teaching languages will be pitched straight into more complex grammatical constructions. It is extremely important that UKS2 teachers plan carefully what constructions and vocabulary they intend to use and, crucially, what constructions and vocabulary the children need to learn and employ. Ensure also that any other adults are fully cognizant with what is required of them in terms of using the target language if they are working with individuals or groups. Using scripts is fine, but keep them short; don't be too ambitious, and remember that support is available from the QCDA guidelines as well as the CILT's Primary Languages website. Most schemes provide detailed 'scripts' of what to include for each session. Using mime, exaggerated gestures and visual aids will help to clarify meaning.

| Observations on target language | | | |
|---|---|---|---|
| Use the table below to record your thoughts, observations and evaluations in relation to your own use of the target language | | | |
| **Name:** | **School:** | **Mentor:** | **Class teacher:** |
| Date of session: | Year group: | Context of session: (i.e. discrete, embedded, own class, other class, after-school club) | |
| Where was my use of the TL successful? (specify) | | | |
| Did children fully understand instructions and objectives? | | | |
| Did I revisit and review TL from previous sessions? | | | |
| Did I allow children enough time to respond? | | | |
| Did I allow children enough time to reflect after making errors? | | | |
| Did I ensure that their errors helped them to learn and to use correct language? Did I then give children the opportunity to use correct language? | | | |
| Did I address misunderstandings and misconceptions? | | | |
| Did I provide enough opportunities for children to use the TL? | | | |
| Did I anticipate correctly the TL the children would need for the lesson? If not, what would have been useful to add? | | | |
| Did I anticipate the TL I would need for the lesson? If not, what would have been useful to add? | | | |
| Did I include assessment opportunities for children's TL use? | | | |
| Did I use praise words enough in the TL? | | | |
| Did I reinforce key words through visual aids/mime/ gesture/display? | | | |
| Was my pronunciation accurate? What do I need to practise? | | | |
| Other thoughts and reflections on the use of TL in this session | | | |

*Figure 2.3* Observations on target language pro forma

Teachers may have fears about using the target language. Moreover, in their own language learning experience their teacher might not have used the target language, and so the relevance of its use is not understood. Not knowing when or how to use the target language may also be a problem. There are many teachers who have a good knowledge of another language but don't speak in it!

The target language is never going to be an easy area for the non-specialist, but with the right help and support it can, hopefully, be viewed in a more positive light and more teachers will be encouraged to attempt it.

## Questioning to promote learning

All teachers are aware of the importance of questioning to promote learning. They know about open questions, closed questions and higher-order questioning. However, questioning for second-language learning is specific and requires other considerations.

Asking open questions when children are beginning to learn another language is not appropriate because children will not have sufficient vocabulary or knowledge of the language to express themselves meaningfully.

The key elements to take into account are as follows:

- Model questions and answers several times before asking the children to respond.
- Allow children sufficient thinking time before answering – they will take longer to formulate an answer in the second language than in their mother tongue.
- Ask the whole class first, then groups, then individuals. It is a good strategy to ask children to raise their hand when they feel ready to answer a question individually.
- Ensure that all children have an opportunity to respond, thus encouraging an inclusive learning environment.
- Ensure that children are able to ask as well as to answer questions.

Asking questions and responding to them should both be emphasised from the outset. Even if children may be initially unsure of what the question means, they should be able to detect a question by the tone of voice used.

An example of extending questioning and pronoun knowledge in LKS2 could be as follows:

Q:  Comment tu t'appelles (*or* Comment t'appelles-tu?)
A:  Je m'appelle . . .

Once children are secure with this, move to a girl in the class and say: 'Comment elle s'appelle? Elle s'appelle . . .'. Next, repeat to a boy: 'Comment il s'appelle? Il s'appelle . . .'.

Model this several times with girls and boys and then ask the class what they notice. They should comment on the il/elle and make the link between he/she. This is an effective way of enabling children to progress from simply asking each other their own names. This can also be extended when learning about family members:

Q:  Tu as une sœur?
R:  Oui, j'ai une sœur
Q:  Comment elle s'appelle?
R:  Elle s'appelle . . .

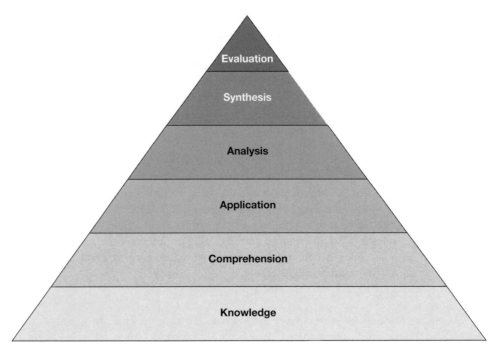

*Figure 2.4* Bloom's taxonomy of learning. Adapted from Bloom, B.S. (ed.) *Taxonomy of educational objectives: the classification of educational goals. Handbook I, cognitive domain* (New York, Toronto: Longmans, Green, 1956).

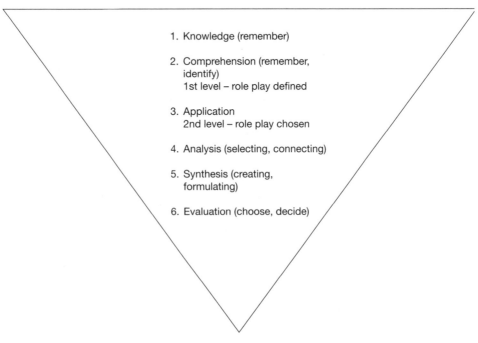

1. Knowledge (remember)

2. Comprehension (remember, identify)
   1st level – role play defined

3. Application
   2nd level – role play chosen

4. Analysis (selecting, connecting)

5. Synthesis (creating, formulating)

6. Evaluation (choose, decide)

*Figure 2.5* Adaptation of Bloom's Taxonomy for language learning: questioning

Bloom's Taxonomy (Figure 2.4) is a well-known and well-used model for developing higher-order thinking and eliciting responses to higher-order questioning.

How, though, can this model be adapted in order to help children to develop higher-order questioning, responses and thinking in another language? The model is wholly appropriate for mother-tongue users, but how appropriate is it for learning a second language when vocabulary, knowledge and syntax are lacking? One way to modify it might be as in Figure 2.5.

How can this approach be applied practically in a lesson? Figure 2.6 shows a possible model.

If planned and implemented properly, questioning allows for assessment of effective teaching and learning. Good questioning should engage and focus the learner. The more this is carried out in Primary Language learning, the more children can have the opportunity to combine the development of cognitive learning skills and linguistic competence.

| Competence | Skills demonstrated |
|---|---|
| **Knowledge** | (Image shown; props used by teacher) |
| 'Il y a du soleil'<br>'Il neige'<br>'Il pleut' | Children repeat phrase and link image/visual demonstration with phrase<br>Language learning strategies: – repetition, visual clues, remembering |
| **Comprehension** | |
| Question: Quel temps fait-il?<br>Response: Il y a du soleil, il neige, il pleut | (Question asked, response shown for each weather type with visual aids and props)<br>Children repeat question as a class and as individuals when **ready to respond**<br>Children respond to question with different weather types prompted by images<br>Children are engaged in 1st level role-play questioning with teacher – question and answer **defined** by teacher<br>*Children repeat, remember and identify* |
| **Application** | |
| Question: Quel temps fait-il?<br>Response  Il y a du soleil, il neige, il pleut | Children are engaged in 2nd level role play – children use question independently and choose answers from visual stimuli presented in pairs<br>*Children repeat, remember, identify, select* |
| **Analysis** | |
| Question: Quel temps fait-il ici?<br>Response: Il y a du soleil | Children are shown postcards/pictures of sunny scenes, for example, Spain or south of France<br>*Children remember, select, connect* |

*Figure 2.6* Model of higher-order questioning in language learning

continued . . .

**Synthesis**

| | |
|---|---|
| Question: C'est quel pays?<br>Response: C'est l'Espagne<br>Question: Quel temps fait-il ici?<br>Response: En Espagne il y a toujours du soleil,<br>  *or* Il y a du soleil souvent en Espagne. | Children are shown maps of France and Spain and asked to identify the name of the country. They are given a choice of words of which they have prior knowledge: e.g. **souvent** (often), **quelquefois** (sometimes), **toujours** (always).<br>They have prior knowledge of names of countries.<br>*Children remember, identify, select, create and formulate responses* |

**Evaluation**

| | |
|---|---|
| Children choose questions, decide countries, decide weather from a selection of maps, words and visual stimuli; this can include beaches, sports pictures (both sun and snow).<br>Qu'est-ce que tu as fait en vacances/en France?<br>J'ai fait . . .<br>(Note: although these are past tenses it is not necessary at this point to labour tenses; rather, give children the tools to be able to converse).<br>Qu'est-ce que tu préfères? Tu préfères le ski ou le snowboard?<br>Je préfère . . . | Children decide questions to ask.<br>Children can formulate responses from their own knowledge – for example, some children may know that there is snow in France and refer to snow sports and areas in France where they know there is snow.<br>It will be necessary to anticipate words/sentence structures/questions that children may need to extend their sentence skills.<br>For example: 'Il neige dans la région des Alpes en France.' 'J'ai fait du ski et du snowboard.' 'Je préfère le ski.'<br>*Children remember, identify, select, connect, create, formulate, decide, compare* |

*Figure 2.6 . . . continued*

## Reflection

- What is my attitude to using the target language when teaching Primary Languages?
- Do I allow children enough time to respond when teaching generally?
- Am I using errors as a focus for learning?
- How can I develop children's phonological awareness when teaching Primary Languages and make links to their phonic knowledge?
- Am I planning questions which will develop higher-order thinking?

# Chapter 3

# The planning and teaching of Primary Languages

This chapter will consider:

- the KS2 Framework for Languages – implications for planning and the framework in practice;
- oracy – speaking and listening;
- literacy – reading and writing;
- language learning strategies – key issues and understanding for non-specialists;
- knowledge about language;
- the importance of linking literacy to primary language learning;
- QCDA guidelines – past and present;
- plenaries (rounding off/summarisation at the end of lessons).

## The KS2 Framework for Languages – implications for planning

When teachers were first confronted with the KS2 Framework for Languages, their immediate reaction was to throw their hands up in horror at yet another weighty tome to be referred to. Five years on, however, the Framework has 'come of age' and provides the key to good and complete delivery of a curriculum for Primary Languages. It is not prescriptive but it does offer clear learning objectives for progression throughout KS2, as well as sample teaching activities and planning guidance. The examples cited for each of the strands have all been tried and tested and are, as such, case studies for using the Framework. In its report entitled *Modern Languages – Achievements and Challenge 2007–2010*, published in January 2011, Ofsted stated that:

> The curriculum in the **outstanding** schools was characterised by:
>
> - the Key Stage 2 Framework used as the main tool for planning . . .
>
> (p. 14)

It also stated that:

> the large majority of the schools visited had planned their provision using the Key Stage 2 Framework or the QCDA's schemes of work (which are **based on the Framework** and the **five strands of primary language learning**). At least half of them used commercial schemes of work **based on the Framework** which were supported by local authorities that provided training in how to use them.

It is clear that schools are relying on the Framework a great deal for support and that it does indeed provide that support. Many schools have taken advantage of the CILT National Primary Languages Training which is based on the Framework's learning strands (see Figure 3.1) and learning objectives.

### The Framework strands

The three core strands of the Framework are Oracy, Literacy and Intercultural Understanding, with two cross-cutting strands – Knowledge about Language and Language Learning Strategies. These can be represented as shown in Figure 3.1 (CILT):

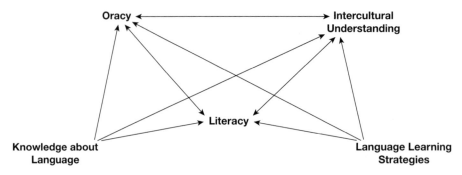

*Figure 3.1* The strands of the KS2 Framework for Languages

## Oracy

I have never been surprised that children at KS3 are quickly turned off learning languages. I am sure that there are many excellent and passionate language teachers, but, with the introduction of speaking, listening, reading and writing all at once when children begin learning a new language, it is hardly surprising that they think 'Too hard', become uninterested and switch off. The key to learning a language is first, listening and second, speaking. Babies listen for a long time before they attempt to utter – but they understand an awful lot before they begin to speak. Anyone who has lived in another country for any length of time also understands this; listening, assimilating, discerning sounds, understanding are all prerequisites to speaking another language. A relative of mine was a classic 'hate languages' student who couldn't understand why she was being made to learn and, what was more, found it totally baffling. When she went to live and work in Belgium at the age of 22 she quickly found herself listening intently to everything, and two years on spoke French fluently. She is now a passionate advocate of language learning. What happened? She saw the relevance most definitely, but more importantly she was **able** to learn because she was exposed to listening to the language constantly and, moreover, **had** to listen in order to understand.

Obviously, it is impossible to mirror living in another country in the classroom, but during LKS2 it is possible to put the emphasis on speaking and listening rather than the written word. In this way children can begin to assimilate grammatical concepts naturally.

For example, children soon pick up on gender difference simply through statements such as: 'j'aime **le** coca, je n'aime pas **la** salade'. They will realise that **je** means **I** through responding to questions – 'comment tu t'appelles?' '**Je** m'appelle . . .' **if they are given the opportunity to practise enough.** In my many conversations with trainees and teachers over the years it is clear that not enough opportunity is given to learners to speak the language or to **ask** questions as well as answer them.

The oracy objectives in the Framework are designed to ensure that children progress, and teachers are provided with sample teaching activities within each objective. This is also true for the literacy objectives, as well as for the intercultural understanding objectives.

It may be helpful to look at particular oracy objectives and, together with examples, at how children can achieve the progression indicated across the Key Stage.

### Year 3: O3.3 Perform simple communicative tasks using single words, phrases and short sentences

I have already mentioned how important it is for children to be able to both ask and answer questions. Different schools will have different models for the delivery of Primary Languages, but whatever the model, review and consolidation of previous vocabulary is vital. The more opportunity children have to listen and engage, the better.

When introducing a new word, phrase or sentence it is important to make it as lively as possible. Teaching children how to respond to the question 'What is your name?' (French: 'Comment tu t'appelles?') is a good starting point. Point to yourself and walk around the classroom saying, 'Je m'appelle . . .' several times. Make sure that you engage the children with eye contact and monitor any child who looks confused. Then ask the question to the whole class and perform a pointing action with each 'Comment tu t'appelles?' Encourage the children to join in with 'Je m'appelle . . .' and then indicate that you want them to say their own name collectively. A whole-class response reduces any feelings of uncertainty and encourages children when they hear others making the same response. Do this a few times, monitoring when you feel that most children have understood. Using the target language together with gestures is helpful, but if you feel that children do not understand, by all means give instructions in English – but continue to ask the question in the target language. Once you are happy with the collective response, ask children the question individually, choosing a child who you know will be confident in responding and telling the children that when they are ready to respond individually to the question they can raise their hand and you will ask them. You may think, 'Do I have to ask every child this question? This will take forever.' And the answer is, 'Yes, you do.' When children are listening to their peers giving their responses, their confidence will increase – and they won't be bored. Far from it; they will be building and reinforcing their understanding. I have never taught a class where all children have not eventually raised their hand and wanted to respond. This approach demonstrates to them that you are treating them as individual learners and that you want to encourage them to speak and understand from the outset. This approach can also be used successfully in KS1, even in the Foundation Stage.

This question/answer can be extended to include others in a role-play scenario that will lead to progression to the **Year 4: O4.4 Ask and answer questions on several topics.** Such questions could be 'Where do you live/I live?' 'How old are you?' 'Do you have any brothers or sisters?' 'Yes, I have . . . brother(s)/sister(s).' 'What is his/her name?' 'What are their names?' etc. Within these questions it can be seen that the gender concept will be raised and children can be asked, for example, to listen out for **il/elle** and identify it in phrases. I have always found that the best way for children to understand the **il/elle s'appelle** grammatical construction is to relate it to the class. Choose a boy (or girl) first and say, 'Il s'appelle . . .'. Children will immediately understand this because they know the child's name. Then move on to a girl and say, 'Elle s'appelle . . .'. Move back to the first child and ask, 'Comment il s'appelle?' to elicit the response, 'Il s'appelle . . .'. (This will need to be modelled initially.) Then go to the girl and say, 'Comment elle s'appelle?' to elicit the response, 'Elle s'appelle . . .'.

When children are secure with the question and response and have practised it several times, ask them what they notice about the two different phrases to elicit 'il/elle . . .' and thus an introduction to the gender concept in language learning. It is much simpler for children to relate a grammatical construction to a concept that is familiar to them.

### Year 5: 05.3 Listen attentively and understand more complex phrases and sentences, and 05.2 Understand and express simple opinions

Activities that will develop children's understanding of more complex phrases may be related to, for example, description of what other children are wearing, which could include adjectives and gender/plural agreement, e.g. 'What is he wearing?' (French: Qu'est-ce qu'il porte?) 'He is wearing a blue shirt, white shorts, red socks and white trainers.' (French: Il porte une chemise bleue, un short blanc, des chaussettes rouges et des baskets blancs.) Another example could be comparison of weather, and compound sentences. 'It's raining here but it is sunny in the south of France.' (French: Il pleut ici mais dans le sud de la France, il y a du soleil.) Use of the phrase 'j'aime/je n'aime pas' can be applied to this objective – discussion of food is always popular, especially if there are samples to try! Demonstrating 'j'aime' or 'je n'aime pas' and then inviting children's responses will give the children good practice in developing and consolidating understanding, and they can progress to starting to justify their dislikes. E.g. 'Je n'aime pas le café au lait parce que je n'aime pas le lait.' Consolidation through song, using well-known melodies, is also helpful.

> J'aime les pommes, J'aime le pain, J'aime le poisson,
> J'aime les fraises, J'aime les frites, C'est vrai!
> J'aime le thé, J'aime le vin, J'aime le coca,
> mais je n'aime pas le café au lait!
> DÉGOÛTANT! ECOEURANT! HORRIBLE!
> Et ça me rend malade.
> DÉGOÛTANT! ECOEURANT!
> Moi, je préfère la salade.
> (To the tune of Sing Hosanna)

### Year 6: 06.3 Understand longer and more complex phrases and sentences

Children can justify further their likes and dislikes – using food, for example: 'I don't like salad because at school it is always horrible. It is always warm and limp.' (French: Je n'aime pas la salade parce que à l'école c'est toujours affreuse. C'est toujours chaude et molle.)

They can also progress to engaging in conversations. A partner school is the ideal forum for children to develop this skill, perhaps through video-conferencing or an exchange visit. This approach will demonstrate the relevance of learning a language if pupils are able to talk to the counterpart children about their own experiences and are also able to ask questions of their counterparts in another country.

### Planning for oracy sessions

In planning for discrete oracy sessions it is helpful to think about children's prior learning, the target language to be used, new vocabulary and grammatical constructions, plus timings. The lesson should take on a similar format to a discrete phonics session, i.e. revisit/review/ teach/practise/apply. The session plan in Figure 2.2 is one used by trainees at my university and which takes into account essential considerations for lesson planning. It can also be used for a language session that is being used for consolidation from a discrete session in another subject area. Figure 2.1 shows a weekly plan which reflects a similar approach to a weekly phonics plan. 'Target language' can mean just single-word instructions – it doesn't necessarily mean using lengthy phrases. Using phrases and sentences can be worked towards and seen as further professional development; it is much better to use single words accurately than sentences that are inaccurate. A good example of this can be seen on the CILT's Primary Languages website. Here a teacher is giving instructions for a PE warm-up session. She does not use any sentences, just one- or two-word instructions, and the children understand perfectly what they have to do. The lesson can be accessed at www.primarylanguages. org.uk/training_zone/teachers/embedding/cross-curricular_links/movement.aspx.

## Literacy – reading and writing

The introduction of reading and writing can be contentious. There are some who advocate not introducing any literacy activities during LKS2 and others who are perfectly happy to have some written words displayed and referred to from the outset.

I am of the latter persuasion; I see no harm at all in children's being able to see the names of everyday objects, phrases and words on display. It is perhaps not advantageous for children to write much during LKS2 (although they are often very keen to do so, and this can be encouraged), but becoming familiar with how words are written and the discrepancies in pronunciation is helpful and important. When using flashcards, progression can be made from pupils' first naming a picture, then looking at the picture and reading the word, until finally the word is shown and they can read and identify meaning. Games with flashcards can be used far more successfully than just showing a picture and inviting a response. Examples of flashcard games include:

- Consolidating understanding of alphabets: children spell out their name with the flashcards.
- Have two sets of flashcards and use them in team games, perhaps by asking 'Qui a . . .?' The first team to show the correct answer gains a point.
- Put children in small groups; place groups of flashcards randomly around the room and say a word. The first child or team to find the correct flashcard gains a point.

- True or false: say the name of the picture on the card (or another name) and ask whether it is true or false.
- Ask children to copy how you say the word, e.g. in a whisper, very loudly, singing.
- Give the flashcards to groups of children and let them take the teacher's role by asking each other.
- Have six or eight children at the front of the class and say, 'Montrez-moi . . .' (or the equivalent in whichever language you are teaching). Children have to point to or say the name of the child with the correct flashcard. You could adapt this in PE by fixing the cards to the walls of the hall and having the children run to the correct flashcard (this game needs very clear ground rules!).
- A very quick starter game when children are orally secure with the vocabulary and are familiar with the written form is simply to hold up the flashcard and ask children to write the word for the picture on individual whiteboards. This is a good way to formatively assess children's spelling knowledge as well as their understanding.
- Noughts and crosses can be played by matching words to pictures. Pin up the cards in noughts and crosses format and pin the corresponding words randomly at the side; children have to match the words to the pictures, and if they are successful can put a nought or cross in the appropriate square.
- Interactive whiteboard (IWB) activities. The following are examples of good websites for such activities:

  www.studystack.com/flashcard-180483#
  http://spanishflashcards.tripod.com/
  www.hello-world.com/German/worksheets/flashcards.php

- Crosswords are an enjoyable way for children to consolidate reading and word-recognition skills. The following website is a nice one which has crosswords in French and English (children have either to read the clue in French and give the English word, or vice versa). It is divided into topics and is in other languages as well as French: www.studystack.com/crossword-180483. Of course it is easy to devise your own crosswords, but every little helps! An extension of this game would be to have the clues in simple sentences, then more complex, which would achieve progression across the Key Stage.

All of the above games can be adapted to progress in reading and writing the vocabulary. Again, it will be helpful to look at specific literacy objectives in order to gain an understanding of the progression that can be achieved across the Key Stage.

### Year 3: L3.1 Recognise some familiar words in written form

Sub-headings for this objective are:

- Understand words displayed in the classroom.
- Identify and read simple words.
- Read and understand simple messages.

Having instructions and everyday items and objects displayed around the classroom and referring to them whilst teaching will enable teachers to achieve this objective readily. It is also an opportunity for cross-curricular work. For example, in Geography, children can refer in the target language to maps on which the names of countries and towns are displayed; directions are also a good thing to display in an interactive format, and children can develop their understanding of map reading by answering questions that are pinned up. In Art, when looking at the work of various artists, colours and names can be referred to. In History, the names of historical figures can be referred to, as well as, perhaps, modes of travel. If, for example, children are studying the Tudors, vocabulary for ships/sea/sky/people could be displayed (Spanish Armada). In PE, instead of saying instructions, you can hold up cards for the children to read. In Numeracy, numbers can be displayed on a language display board, as well as greetings and common class events such as birthdays and holidays. The use of flashcards and the IWB have already been discussed. Children could also communicate with each other by sending simple postcards or letters, e.g. 'Cher Pierre, il fait beau, amities Jean', which is a literacy objective for Year 3.

### Year 4: Read and understand a range of familiar written phrases

Match phrases and short sentences to pictures or themes.

Identify non-fiction texts by their style and layout, e.g. a recipe, a weather forecast, instructions for making and doing something, a letter, an advertisement.

The flashcard games already discussed would be appropriate for achieving the first objective, but the concept could be adapted to any topic or subject area and used in a range of activities, for example, a daily routine to consolidate time vocabulary (see Figure 3.2). In addition, the following are useful activities:

- Any kind of drag-and-drop activity on the IWB.
- Have a box with different objects and have the names of them on labels. Children can take it in turns to take something out of the box and ask the rest of the class the question 'Qu'est-ce que c'est?' (This can be displayed on the IWB or whiteboard.) Children can then write the phrase 'C'est un . . .' on individual whiteboards and hold them up. This can, of course, be adapted for any language that is being taught.
- Have a set of pictures with phrases underneath that have to be matched to the appropriate activity.
- An activity for Geography could be to have a map of France with some towns located on it and to ask children to write where the towns are, in response to questions. E.g. 'Où est Lille?' 'Lille est dans le nord de la France.'

The second sub-heading for this objective offers plenty of opportunity for creative teaching, and teachers should not feel restricted because of their lack of knowledge of the language. A golden rule is to think how you would deliver the subject area in English and then to adapt. Don't be tempted to use dry, repetitive approaches (of which you may have memories at secondary level) because of lack of confidence; engage with the possibilities, and the children will respond to your enthusiasm. Make a television frame and have children starring in it, saying the weather forecast in French with props. Even better, video them doing it. Make hot chocolate, a Black Forest cake, tapas, or even bake some croissants from scratch!

| | |
|---|---|
|  | A 7 heures, je me lève. |
|  | A 9 heures je vais à l'école. |
|  | A midi je mange le déjeuner. |
|  | A minuit je dors. |
|  | A 8 heures moins le quart je mange mon petit déjeuner. |

*Figure 3.2* Sequencing activity to consolidate time vocabulary

### Year 5: L5.1 Re-read frequently a variety of short texts

- Read fiction and non-fiction texts, e.g. extracts from stories, email messages and texts from the internet.

Email messages are particularly appropriate for children to learn from because email correspondence and social networking sites are such an integral part of their lives, as is the internet generally. As previously mentioned, correspondence via email with a partner school is invaluable in this context because the children will be writing and reading for a purpose. Children can use their ICT skills to further their geographical knowledge of their partner school's region and activities can be built round their research, e.g. making a tourist brochure – which could be a reciprocal activity.

Looking at, for example, French shopping catalogue websites is an excellent way for children to consolidate and extend vocabulary and can be used for extension activities, especially in Numeracy. Such activities can be adapted for all languages studied.

It is appropriate to introduce dictionaries at this stage because children will want to look up words that they may need when writing emails to their partner schools.

It may be that at this stage a visit is planned within the school programme, which offers many opportunities for communication and research (as detailed in Chapter 6).

### Year 6: L6.1 Read and Understand the main points and some detail from a short written passage

- Read and respond to, e.g., an extract from a story, an email message or a song.
- Give true or false responses to statements about a written passage.
- Read descriptions of people in the school or class and identify who they are.

It can be seen from the first sub-heading in this objective that progress can be made from Year 5 through writing extended emails and through working independently, rather than through a group or class approach, which is probably more likely in Year 5. A visit to the partner school will create further incentives for children to write, and again gives purpose.

It is interesting to look at books that Year 6-aged children in the partner schools may be reading and to compare them with English literature. This will require children to respond to texts rather than just derive literal meaning from them.

An interesting website is http://e-stories.org/categories.php?&lan=fr&art=s&rid=4, which gives categories of short stories in different languages. There are plenty to choose from and they would be useful for Year 6 children to use in different ways. For example, they can skim the text and look for cognates to see if they can get the gist of the story. The text can also be presented to the children and they can work out which genre they think it might be (e.g. fantasy, humour) and give their reasons. Looking at the structure of the language in more depth will develop children's understanding of syntax in the target language as well as in their own. (This aspect is looked at in more depth later in this chapter – the importance of linking literacy to Primary Languages.)

Reading descriptions of people in school (descriptions of teachers are especially liked) is an enjoyable activity and can be extended to writing descriptions of famous people or celebrities. A popular and tried and tested activity entails children working in two teams, and then in pairs within the teams. They have to choose a famous person from a list on a whiteboard that only the teacher can see. The children go one by one to the teacher to choose a name. When a name as been chosen it is rubbed off board. It is necessary to list at least six more names than are actually needed for the activity. Children then write a description and put it in an envelope. The teams swap envelopes and in pairs take it in turns to read out the description to their team. The team has to guess who the celebrity is, and scores a point if it guesses correctly. If the guess is incorrect, the other team scores a point. This activity develops vocabulary knowledge, reading and comprehension skills in the target language, as well as listening skills generally.

It is possible for Year 6 children to reach a good level in the target language, but teachers should not feel anxious about this because it is a level that they too can attain easily if they take opportunities to upskill, if the school uses good resources and, above all, if a positive and enthusiastic approach is demonstrated to the children.

## Intercultural understanding (IU)

This is examined in depth in Chapter 6, but some progression aspects will be looked at here.

### Year 3 IU3.1 Learn about the different languages spoken by children in the school

- Increase awareness of linguistic and cultural diversity.

It is vital that our children become aware of and accept cultural and linguistic diversity. Learning another language is an ideal vehicle for development of this tolerance. Children with other languages and from other cultures are a rich resource in schools by which to achieve this. Simple approaches, such as displaying the geographical location of children's countries, key language phrases that can be taught to all the children and the acknowledgement and discovery of celebrations will all contribute to a true and welcoming multicultural school ethos.

This approach will obviously also be used for the target-language country/countries. Children need to know that French is spoken not just in France and Spanish is spoken not only in Spain!

### Year 4: IU4.4 Learn about ways of travelling to the country/countries

To progress from the Year 3 objective, children can research for themselves in which countries their target language is spoken and consider how those countries can be reached. This can be linked to PSHCE and the Environment: children can research the most eco-friendly way to travel. They can also research costs and compare the cheapest and most expensive ways of travelling to the countries concerned.

### Year 5: IU5.1 Look at further aspects of their everyday lives from the perspective of someone from another country

Two of the *Every Child Matters* outcomes for children – enjoying and achieving both their full potential and economic well-being – can be furthered through acquiring language skills.

Prospective employers are always impressed when an applicant has knowledge of other languages. Having a broad knowledge and insight into other countries' cultures and lifestyles can be nothing but beneficial. The IU objectives encourage children to delve more deeply into their own country's culture and to consider cultural issues. A sub-heading of this learning objective is for children to 'reflect on cultural issues using empathy and imagination to understand other people's experiences'. What does this mean, exactly? The Framework advises teachers to look at the communication skills needed for when 'non-native speakers' visit a class – factors such as 'intonation and gesture' should be considered as well as 'speaking slowly'. This is helpful for children, and other aspects should also be emphasised, such as direct eye contact and positive body language. All of these skills are extremely important for children to develop throughout their school career because they contribute towards a confident attitude and to becoming a well-rounded individual.

### Year 6: IU6.2 Recognise and understand some of the differences between people

When learning about other countries, it is sometimes difficult for children not to have stereotypical ideas about how people look, what they wear, the food they eat etc. This was reinforced for me when children came to school in fancy dress on European Days. I lost count of the numbers of striped tops and berets and flamenco dresses. The very notion of having children come to school in fancy dress invites stereotypical outfits, but such outfits are also a celebration of each country's culture. Should this be included or not? The subject is an interesting one for debate both in the class and in the staff room. Would we want our own country to be represented in a stereotypical manner on equivalent days in a European school that is studying English? Beefeater outfits and kilts might just be acceptable, but what if children turned up for the day carrying lager cans and shouting loudly in groups? The world-wide media has often represented our country negatively, and we should not be surprised if people in other countries think that the majority in our country behave in such away. This provides all the more reason for us to engage and talk as much as possible with our European counterparts, so that we may understand each other's cultures to the extent possible. Stereotypical views should be challenged through open discussion, in order to ensure that they are not founded on racism or prejudice. It is important to look at similarities as well as differences.

## Language learning strategies

> Foreign or second language (L2) learning strategies are specific actions, behaviors, steps, or techniques students use – often consciously – to improve their progress in apprehending, internalizing, and using the L2.
>
> (Oxford, 1990)

This quotation applies to adult learners, but is no less relevant to younger learners. However, it could be argued that with child learners the strategies are directed by the teacher and are **adopted** by the learner. There has been much research into the exact nature of language learning strategies (LLS), notably by Rubin (1975) and Stern (1975), which focuses on the 'importance of the strategies used by learners in the language learning process' and asserts that the 'students are the only ones that can do the learning'. This is true to the extent that, when asked for a response in another language, it is only the learner who can assimilate his or her knowledge and put it into practice. Perhaps an analogy can be made with the driving test. Anyone who has taken a driving test knows that it is solely down to the driver whether they drive the car successfully or not. (Whether they pass and the reasons why they fail are perhaps more contentious, and can be considered to be more arbitrary!) What comes out of a person's mouth, however, they alone are responsible for, and the development of that knowledge is also, to a large extent, their sole responsibility. This is not to say, of course, that teachers do not have an impact on children's language learning; but **how** they learn is tremendously important. This could perhaps be one of the reasons why language learning is traditionally viewed as one of the harder subjects, and why it is viewed so negatively in this country.

LLS are 'behaviors or thoughts that a learner engages in during . . . the learner's encoding process' (Weinstein and Mayer, 1986, 315). These strategies 'are the techniques for the learner's **conscious** construction of language rules, vocabulary, pronunciation, discourse, and sociocultural understanding' (ibid., 315)

The key aspects of language learning feature throughout the Framework – rhyme, memorisation, looking at the face and mouth of the person who is speaking, repetition, looking for visual and aural clues, and practice – and all are essential strategies to employ. For non-specialists and non-language learners, most of these strategies will be new in this context, but they will also be completely familiar to the primary teacher, particularly in teaching phonics and reading. The fact that primary teachers will recognise and be comfortable with these strategies should be emphasised to reticent language learners in order to build confidence.

## Knowledge about language

Chomsky's theory of language's being innate, that knowledge of language is predetermined, that there is a 'Universal Grammar' has been controversial, but nevertheless it is acknowledged within the Framework that children should be able to recognise patterns and apply their syntactic knowledge to support their understanding of both the spoken and the written word. This assumption goes some way to supporting Chomsky's theory and the fact that children can refer back to the syntactic structure of their native tongue in order to somehow understand the order of the language being learned – even if that order is different. The fact that it is different can reinforce their syntactic understanding of their mother tongue. These are extremely complex notions and relate to Chomsky's hypotheses of the 'Deep' and 'Surface' structure of language.

In addition to syntax rules, knowledge about language extends to phonic knowledge, writing systems, intonation, word classes, politeness conventions and cognates.

It is important that children understand that many languages 'work' in a similar way. There is a view that if children learn one language at primary school and then go to secondary school where they learn an entirely different language, this is somehow detrimental. On the contrary, it can be argued that, by having already studied a language successfully at primary level, children have an insight into how languages 'work' and will approach learning another language with confidence. Of course it is helpful to be able to build on language knowledge at secondary level, but I don't feel that it is disastrous to learn a different language, and in many ways it can be an advantage. Children should see languages as an integral part of the curriculum, and four years of language learning should pave the way to enthusiasm and self-belief.

## The importance of linking literacy to Primary Language learning

The Literacy Framework and the KS2 Framework for Languages are closely linked and the interrelationship of the Framework objectives to the literacy objectives is evident.

Aside from the Framework, however, the objectives for good literacy teaching link closely to good language teaching. Children need to be able to communicate effectively, which means that they should be able to listen with discernment and to respond articulately. It is necessary to both look at and listen to the speaker intently when learning another language. These are skills that need to be learned for life and that are complemented by learning another language. Developing listening skills is crucial to all areas of learning and, as they improve, children's concentration spans will also improve. The foundations of language learning include rhyme, repetition and rhythm – all strategies that are essential to foreign language learning. Grammar awareness also develops through listening and exposure to language patterns. There is no need to explain to a child after a term of saying twice weekly 'Je m'appelle . . .' that 'Je' means 'I'; they will have absorbed and assimilated that knowledge. As the Department for Education states in its National Strategies document *Developing Language in the Primary School: Literacy and Primary Languages*: 'The Early Learning Goals as identified in the EYFS (Early Years Foundation Stage) CLL (Communication, Language and Literacy) Framework bear a remarkable resemblance to the skills children need to acquire proficiency in a new language.'

In acquiring their own language, children

- Learn to listen and discriminate sounds, developing their aural comprehension span
- Are given time to talk, thus developing vocabulary, syntax, intonation and awareness of audience
- Are given opportunities to listen to music and develop rhythm, voice control and articulation
- Listen to stories and become familiar with language and grammar
- Develop understanding of the written word
- Develop phonological awareness
- Develop understanding of writing.

(Department for Education, 2009)

Children's learning development in the early stages mirrors the acquisition of a second language, and learning a second language supports and extends their knowledge and understanding of their own language.

Extremely complex, almost instantaneous thought processes are involved in learning the syntax of another language. Children consider the new construction, relate it to their own language and check the word order, then go back to the new language and consider how it is different to their own before applying it. This occurs when they are secure in the new construction and capable of comparison. Clearly, none of this is articulated, but it occurs nonetheless. When speakers who have lived in another country and spoken another language for any length of time then converse in their mother tongue, they often translate literally from the other language and self-correct. Learning another language, then, can provide an opportunity for the syntax of the mother tongue to be reinforced.

As Johann Wolfgang von Goethe (1749–1832), German writer, scientist and master of poetry, drama and the novel wrote, 'A man who does not know a foreign language is ignorant of his own' (*Wer fremde Sprachen nicht kennt, weiß nichts von seiner eigenen*).

## QCDA guidelines for languages at KS2

The QCDA legacy of the schemes of work for languages at KS2 will stand schools in good stead in delivering the Entitlement for Languages because they enable schools to deliver the objectives of the KS2 Framework for Languages.

The activities and ideas are appropriate for KS2 and the subject area 'feels' primary rather than a watered-down version of secondary content. The emphasis is on learning through stories, games and song, but not at the expense of progression. Although the QCDA website is now defunct, many schools will have downloaded and have hard copies of the guidelines that they are likely to use until they become confident in their delivery. They are intended for schools and teachers to adapt for their own use. In addition, many local authorities have produced excellent schemes of work which schools also use.

The guidelines can be accessed on the CILT Primary Languages website, as mentioned previously. They are available in French, German, Spanish and Portuguese and consist of 24 units and are accompanied by a Teachers' Guide. The first 12 units are intended for LKS2 and units 13–24 for UKS2. However, if a school has introduced languages from KS1, the first units can be easily adapted for younger children. Indeed, introducing languages at KS1 offers teachers the opportunity to develop children's phonological awareness and to link foreign language learning with phonics acquisition, the isolation of phonemes, recognising letter patterns, discerning sounds and the use of song, rhyme and repetition.

As with other QCDA guidelines, the scheme of work covers long- and medium-term planning and offers suggestions for short-term planning. The Teachers' Guide emphasises a teaching sequence of presentation (delivery), practice (activities) and production (performance, written work, displays etc.). The guide offers many useful suggestions for the primary practitioner, and sound advice for the non-specialist.

The TDA has also produced a version of the QCDA schemes of work (available from the CILT Primary Languages website) that is specifically aimed at trainees to enable them to have a 'one-stop' reference for Primary Languages planning. It takes into account long-, medium- and short-term plans plus links to the KS2 Framework, prior learning, resources, cross-curricular links, ICT suggestions, follow-up and consolidation throughout the week, embedding opportunities, extension and support ideas.

## Plenaries

The use of plenaries in the discrete (and embedded) language lesson is very important. It offers another opportunity, aside from the initial review and revisit part of the lesson, to consolidate learning and to formatively assess children's learning.

For teachers, the aims of the plenary can perhaps be summarised as follows:

- focus children's awareness of the key concept of the lesson;
- address children's misconceptions and errors, which should then be used as opportunities for learning;
- develop children's confidence in using vocabulary to ask questions about their learning, thus deepening their cognitive understanding;
- consolidate learning;
- assess learning;

- celebrate children's achievements and praise them;
- make use of different teaching and learning styles.

For pupils, the aims of the plenary should be:

- to help them reflect on their learning from the lesson;
- to clarify learning;
- to help them reflect on their progress;
- to demonstrate that errors assist their learning;
- to celebrate their achievements and gain confidence in their learning;
- to self-assess their learning;
- to review prior learning;
- to understand appropriate links to other subject areas.

The plenary offers a golden opportunity for the use of the target language. If it is planned effectively, a plenary can enable both teacher and pupils to use the target language purposefully and successfully. For the non-specialist teacher it can assist consolidation and aid professional development. However, it should not be simply a summing up of the lesson's learning objectives. A good plenary will offer children the prospect of demonstrating their understanding through articulating what they have learned. Very often (and Ofsted's findings support this) the plenary is the weakest part of a lesson, for various reasons:

- there is not enough time and the plenary is rushed;
- if the plenary is not planned it is less likely to be effective;
- questions are not planned with a view to extending (and consolidating) learning;
- there is not enough interaction and too much 'teacher talk'.

Examples of activities for plenaries include:

- role play
- quizzes (using IWB)
- games
- questioning
- songs
- video clips
- discussions
- matching
- sharing, explanations and assessments of work completed in session
- partner work
- children taking on the teacher's role in turns
- pointing, saying and showing, to demonstrate understanding
- written responses (e.g. with individual whiteboards)
- feedback from an activity
- pronunciation practice
- target setting
- providing students with answers (they have to ask the question).

Plenaries should feature regularly in sessions so that an expectation is set up for children to:

- participate
- know that activities will be varied
- know that prior learning will be reviewed as well as new learning.

It is also helpful to refer to learning objectives frequently; the use of mini-plenaries throughout a session is just as valid for Primary Language learning as for other subjects.

Trainees should view plenaries as 'a useful way to help them consider and understand both the structure of lessons . . . and the importance of evaluating and monitoring learning as a component of assessment for learning to inform future teaching' (DCSF 2004).

## Reflection

- Which strands of the Framework am I least confident in delivering? How can I address this?
- How can I develop my teaching to emphasise the links between literacy and language learning?
- Am I using and planning plenaries in the best way to assist children's learning?

# Chapter 4

# Primary Languages across the curriculum

This chapter will consider:

* opportunities for creativity and how different areas of the curriculum can be linked effectively with language learning;
* the use of songs and games to promote effective learning;
* how to embed Primary Languages in the curriculum and the importance of a whole-school ethos;
* Content Language Integrated Learning (CLIL).

## Cross-curricular opportunities and creativity in Primary Languages

What are the cross-curricular opportunities for learning a foreign language in the primary classroom? After due consideration of this question, trainees invariably respond that they can think of no area of the curriculum where languages could not be linked effectively. Clearly, then, there are ample opportunities for primary languages to be reinforced at primary level using teaching strategies with which the primary teacher is familiar and comfortable. Including languages in cross-curricular planning demonstrates to children that the acquisition of language skills and language learning are an integral part of the curriculum. This is vital to assist in changing the attitude that still persists, that languages are not as important as other subjects or are not learnt 'properly' until KS3.

> Making links between curriculum subjects and areas of learning can deepen children's understanding by providing opportunities to reinforce and enhance learning.
>
> (DfES, 2004)

Not only are teachers secure with this approach, but children are too. They are well used to making links between subject areas and are quick to recognise them. Planning lessons that include languages gives children the clear message that learning another language is an important part of the curriculum. The primary class teacher is ideally placed to ensure that the links made are meaningful and will ensure progression. As with other subject areas, teachers can ensure that the programmes of work planned are enjoyable and motivating, but at the same time challenging and relevant to the children. A word of warning, however:

While 'fun and games' are an important part of Modern Foreign Languages and play a major role in motivating pupils, early learners also need to be challenged and to have their learning guided through clear stages of progression if initial motivation is to be maintained.

(Jones and Coffey, 2006: 66)

This can pose problems, particularly if language teaching interrupts another teaching session – perhaps by a native speaker who isn't part of the school's core staff and who comes in for a 'separate' lesson, which is likely to be centred around games and/or singing; or possibly a specialist teacher who does not teach a class within the school and is viewed by the children as detached from the other members of staff. Children can be left with the message: 'that was a fun break, back to work now'. Any additional teachers for Primary Languages, i.e. those other than the regular teaching staff in the school, should be fully conversant with the school's timetable and consult with the class teachers on matters of planning so that they can follow up work wherever possible. If this matter is not addressed, children are less likely to make progress.

It is crucial that, however children are taught Primary Languages, they are challenged sufficiently to match their cognitive ability, to demonstrate progress in their learning and to sustain motivation.

Whilst it is clearly more appropriate to learn vocabulary such as numbers and colours at KS2 rather than at KS3, it is vital to ensure that children are challenged cognitively as well as linguistically. For example, if numbers are being reinforced in a **Numeracy** session during the mental/oral starter, children in Year 3 will quickly learn the numbers up to 20 and beyond, but simply revising the names of the numbers is not enough. Initially, a game such as noughts and crosses (French: Morpion; Spanish: tres en raya; German: Tic Tac Toe) will quickly help in consolidation of numbers. Children can be divided into teams and take turns to choose a number, and also employ strategies to win the game. If one team does not know the answer, the question can be passed to the other team.

This game can be adapted to challenge children appropriately. For example, instead of just putting numbers in the O/X grid (Figure 4.1), consider using calculations in order to reinforce concepts that are appropriate for Year 3 progression, e.g. 2, 5 and 10 times tables and the inverse relationship between multiplication and division (Figure 4.2).

In this way children can reinforce their understanding of numbers in the target language without progression in numeracy being compromised.

When children learn a foreign language they need to acquire new learning strategies precisely because it *is* foreign to them; they need also to develop the ability to meet new challenges. Piaget believed that cognitive development takes place when a child is faced with an idea or experience that does not fit into his or her realm of understanding. Learning a language at primary level, then, offers children opportunities to develop their cognitive and psychological abilities because of the conflict that such learning presents.

Children who are adequately exposed to two languages at an early age experience gains: they are more flexible and creative, and they reach high levels of cognitive development at an earlier age than their monolingual peers.

(Hamayan, 1986)

Hamayan's study relates to dual language instruction specifically, but it is by no means unlikely to suppose also that exposure to another language within the primary education system offers children similar benefits in terms of cognitive and intellectual gain.

| 5 | 11 | 8 |
|---|----|---|
| 19 | 13 | 20 |
| 7 | 18 | 14 |

*Figure 4.1* Grid for simple number consolidation

| $9 \times 2 =$ | $7 \times 2 =$ | $4 \times 5 =$ |
|---|---|---|
| $14 \div 2 =$ | $8 \times 2 =$ | $8 \times 5 =$ |
| $20 \div 5 =$ | $7 \times 10 =$ | $18 \div 2 =$ |

*Figure 4.2* Extension grid to match cognitive development

The following example of a cross-curricular approach taken by one school, based on the North Yorkshire Primary Languages scheme of work, demonstrates how languages can be taught successfully within careful planning, and incorporates looking at 'Healthy Eating' in **Science**.

Year 4 children were initially read the story *The Very Hungry Caterpillar* in French – a story that was well known to all of them. The children, with visual clues, were able to determine the meaning of several words using prior knowledge (days of the week, names of fruits and numbers) and cognates (*oranges, superbes*). Some discrete teaching of days of the week and names of fruits followed. Linking the vocabulary to healthy eating and science, the children were given the opportunity to make their own fruit kebabs – choosing which fruits they would like and asking for them (*je voudrais une fraise, je voudrais une pomme,* etc.) Finally, they drew their finished kebabs, labelled them and ate them! It is important to note that the book is used as a 'way in' to teach the children, but not dwelt upon (clearly, *The Very Hungry Caterpillar* is below the cognitive understanding of Year 4 children). Offering them the opportunity to draw on their knowledge of the book helped them to build confidence in mastering new French vocabulary and syntax and also provided opportunities for cross-curricular teaching. Examples of this work can be seen in Figure 4.3.

Another example relates to **Literacy**. Children were asked to think of animals that they thought they would see in a jungle and then write a list of them, to include numbers and adjectives. Within the task there was a grammatical focus on agreement of gender and singular or plural. The animals could be any colours the children wanted them to be (e.g. deux petits singes marrons et bleus; huit petits toucans roses et oranges) (Figure 4.4).

A further benefit of this exercise was that children considered in depth the syntax of singular and plural in English – looking at the grammatical structure of another language can help to reinforce children's understanding of their own. Speaking, listening, reading and writing skills are all mutually enhancing when children are learning their own language. As discussed in Chapter 3, learning another language can further develop these skills. This activity was extended to making a pop-up book for younger children. The task not only extended the children's linguistic understanding but was also creative and cognitively challenging. It is also cross-curricular link to a Year 4 QCDA unit for **Design and Technology** An example of a pop-up book made is shown in Figure 4.5.

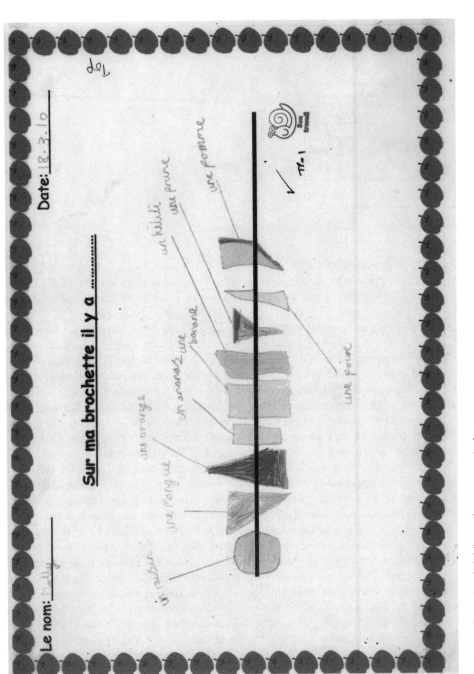

*Figure 4.3a* Example of child's work: cross-curricular

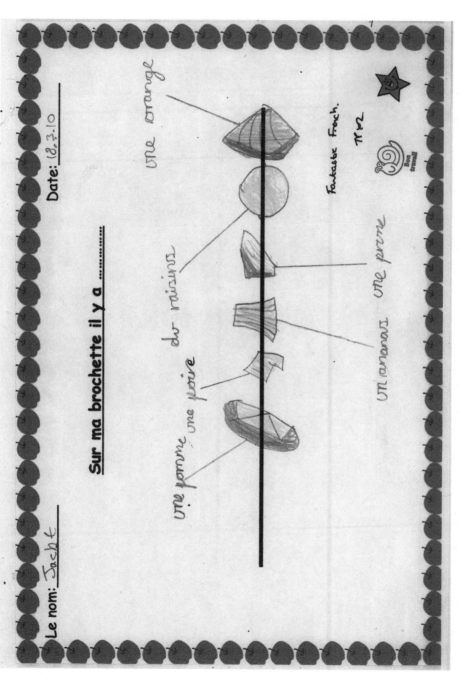

Figure 4.3b Example of child's work: cross-curricular

*Figure 4.3c* Example of child's work: cross-curricular

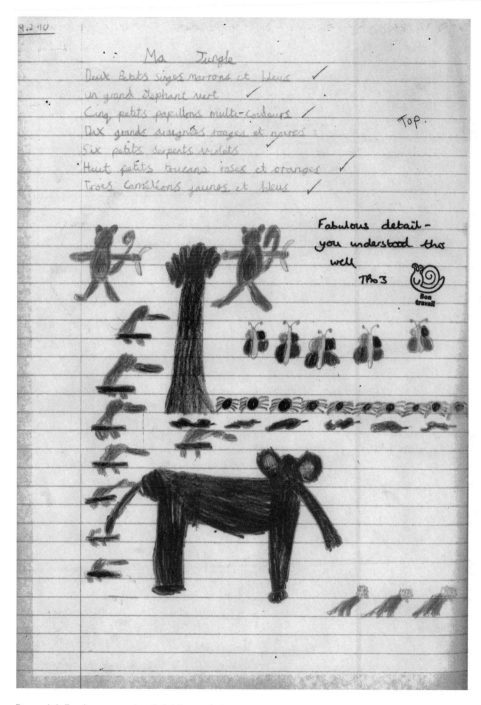

*Figure 4.4* Further example of child's work: literacy

*Figure 4.5a* Example of extension activity in literacy and design and technology

*Figure 4.5b* Example of extension activity in literacy and design and technology

*Figure 4.5c* Example of extension activity in literacy and design and technology

*Figure 4.5d* Example of extension activity in literacy and design and technology

*Figure 4.5e* Example of extension activity in literacy and design and technology

*Figure 4.5f* Example of extension activity in literacy and design and technology

Warm-ups for a literacy lesson can be linked to languages – for example, building sentences: 'Une pomme, une pomme rouge, une pomme rouge et petite, une pomme rouge, petite et ronde', and perhaps looking at phonic patterns, highlighting adjectives and verbs from text or writing. This aspect has been explored in depth in Chapter 3.

Looking at famous artists' styles, part of the **Art and Design** curriculum, affords marvellous opportunities to integrate languages in a cross-curricular approach. Children could consider what they understand art to be, and perhaps draw their thoughts using a mind-map. Figure 4.6 is a Year 7/8 example but could perfectly well be adapted for Year 6. There are many cognates in French that are related to art (la poésie, la musique, les films, la littérature, la photographie etc.).

Colours are another obvious link, but the cross-curricular approach can be extended to incorporate the artists' styles and intercultural understanding. For example, looking at the website of the Musée d'Orsay and its excellent resources will help children to understand the development of the Impressionist movement. It is important for children to have an insight into other artists besides French ones. A Spanish approach might consider the architect Gaudí and his wonderful works in Barcelona. Alternatively, look at www.artcyclopedia.com/nationalities/Spanish.html, which lists Spanish artists and gives examples of their work.

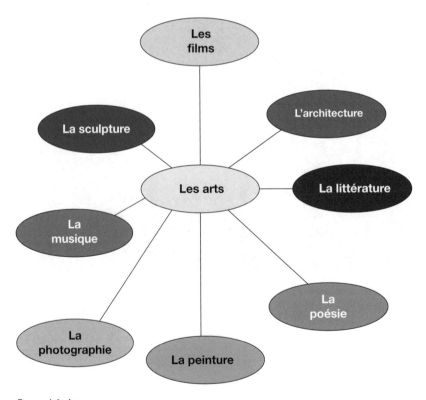

*Figure 4.6* Art cognates

Some schools are now teaching Mandarin, and calligraphy in Chinese characters is a fascinating activity for children. Finding out the children's names in Mandarin (www. mandarintools.com/chinesename.html) can lead to making a wonderful display. Teaching children about the Chinese New Year can be linked to all the artwork that is associated with that celebration. For example, children could make a Chinese dragon by painting and decorating boxes and linking them together with string; some of the children can then hold the boxes just above their heads and dance whilst others perform appropriate percussion-based music. The following site gives many links to activities and teaching about the Chinese New Year: www.activityvillage.co.uk/chinese_new_year.htm. Chinese Scroll paintings also give children a good insight into Chinese artwork: www.thavibu.com/china/index.htm.

**Role Play** is important both in KS1 and KS2, but is somewhat neglected in KS2, possibly because there are still connotations with the 'Home Corner' for KS2 children and it is regarded as babyish. However, role play and art and design can come to the fore together in language learning. Consider an authentic French café; a Spanish tapas restaurant; a German café or Kaffeehaus, which could emphasise the Germans' love for breakfasts, and all the vocabulary that goes with it. Children could design their own menus, décor, practise currency conversion, determine the necessary vocabulary and decide what they feel they need to learn for the role play areas. As with younger children, it is important for the children can take ownership of the role play area and that it is continually developing.

In **PE** there are numerous opportunities for consolidation during warm-ups, e.g. instructions for walking, running, stopping, crawling, jumping can be given. Colours can be put in the four corners of the room and children have to run to the correct colour. This approach could be adapted for most new vocabulary, e.g. using fruits, countries, numbers, family vocabulary.

In **History** the following are possible areas of study:

- The QCDA unit 'Children in World War II' provides scope for foreign language learning. For example, looking at the French Resistance Movement would give children interesting opportunities to consider what it might have been like for a child living with a family who were part of the Resistance.
- Several of Henry VIII's wives had European connections: Catherine of Aragon (Spain), Ann Boleyn (France), Ann of Cleves (Germany). Some research into the countries could be carried out and information displayed and labelled in the appropriate languages.
- The Spanish Armada could be studied, enabling the children to learn vocabulary related to ships and the sea. This could be extended into drama, and a language exchange between Sir Francis Drake and Phillip of Spain.

Cross-curricular links can be used as opportunities to consolidate discrete language learning, or a themed approach can be taken, in which a range of subjects are considered. Tierney and Hope's example of a project on the European Union is often cited as follows:

- Languages: pupils learn names of European countries and their capitals.
- In Geography pupils describe their and others' locations with compass points and revisit geographical features in the foreign language. They use their knowledge of colours to describe flags.
- In Maths they convert currencies.

- In Music pupils learn traditional songs and dances and learn about famous European musicians.
- In Art pupils learn about different artists and their works.
- In Design and Technology pupils prepare some typical European foods.

Another cross-curricular example would be of the children to look at Paris as a theme:

- In ICT software could be used to simulate a take-off, air travel and landing in Paris.
- The children could learn about the famous landmarks of Paris and the vocabulary related to the transport system (le Metro, le tram, les billets, le guichet etc.).
- In Geography children could look at settlements and how Paris grew; vocabulary for rivers and towns could be developed.
- In Design and Technology children could construct models of famous French buildings – e.g. the Eiffel Tower, the Arc de Triomphe, and evaluate their models in French.
- In Art children could have a virtual tour of the Musée d'Orsay or the Louvre and learn vocabulary related to Impressionism and to art generally.
- In RE children could compare religious buildings – e.g. Sacré Coeur, Notre Dame.
- Children could role-play giving directions in French from a map projected on the IWB.
- French café culture could be explored, which is an obvious area for role play.
- French music could be listened to and the French National Anthem learned.
- In History children could learn about the French Revolution and the storming of the Bastille in 1789. There are numerous online images that could be shown to the children for them to gain a sense of the importance of Bastille Day for the French.

Teaching in a cross-curricular way helps to encourage creativity from the teacher's standpoint as well as the children's. Some feel that the prescriptive nature of the curriculum has stifled the primary teacher's natural leanings towards creativity. Most trainees and teachers, if asked, state that being able to teach imaginatively is one of the main reasons why primary teaching attracted them as a career.

Promoting creativity is a powerful way of engaging pupils with their learning.

(DfES, 2003: 31)

Primary Languages enables teachers to be creative in all areas of the curriculum, whilst at the same developing intercultural understanding and providing a global perspective on education.

The following are good websites for developing a cross-curricular approach:

- http://wsgfl.westsussex.gov.uk/ccm/navigation/curriculum/modern-foreign-languages/key-stage-2/cross-curricular-resource-packs/french
- www.bucksgfl.org.uk/course/view.php?id=48
- http://nationalstrategies.standards.dcsf.gov.uk/node/188107
- www.primarylanguages.org.uk/teaching_and_learning/embedding/cross_curricular_links/mini_beasts.aspx.

## Using songs and games to good effect

A curriculum area not discussed in depth thus far is Music. Music and songs benefit children a great deal when learning a foreign language. They provide opportunities to manipulate the language and to become used to pronunciations that may not be familiar to them in their mother tongue.

Asking children to discern and isolate sounds and detect rhythm when listening to songs clearly enhances listening skills in an enjoyable way. The teacher can request physical responses from the children when they have recognised or discerned specific sounds, words or phrases – e.g. standing up, waving, arms in the air, high fives. Pronunciation can be a focus when singing. For example, using the song 'Une poule sur le mur' is an opportunity for children to distinguish between the 'u' and 'ou' sound in French. 'U' is notoriously difficult for the English to pronounce, but it can be approached in a fun way – ask the children to smile and say 'eee', and then ask them to gradually bring their lips together as if they were puckering up to kiss someone. The children should then notice how the 'eee' sound changes to French 'u' pronunciation. Ask them to consider the position of their tongue when saying it, so as to get them used to pronouncing it when they are not going from 'eee' to 'u', but saying it in context.

The chorus of the following song is nonsense ('Picoti Picota'), but children can be asked to pick out the sounds and distinguish them from the other words in the verse:

> Une poule sur le mur
> Qui picotait du pain dur
> Picoti Picota
> Lève la queue et puis s'en va,
> Par ce petit chemin-là

The children may not understand all the words in a song, but this does not detract from their enjoyment, especially when actions are introduced. They can certainly understand the 'gist' and join in repetitive choruses. Children particularly enjoy doing chicken movements during the last two lines, moving round the class and making cockerel noises after the last line!

Songs can be used to consolidate learning from discrete language learning sessions. For example, teaching children the vocabulary for 'pommes', 'pain', 'poissons', 'fraises', 'frites', 'thé', 'vin', 'coca', 'café au lait' alongside the construction 'j'aime/je n'aime pas' can be brought together in the following song (sung to the tune of 'Sing Hosanna'):

### Dégoûtant, Écoeurant

J'aime les pommes, J'aime le pain, J'aime le poisson, J'aime les fraises, J'aime les frites, C'est vrai! J'aime le thé, J'aime le vin, J'aime le coca, mais je n'aime pas le café au lait!

DÉGOÛTANT! ÉCOEURANT! HORRIBLE! Et ça me rend malade. DÉGOÛTANT! ÉCOEURANT! Moi, je préfère la salade.

Devon Learning and Development Partnership has carried out a considerable amount of research into combining songs/language learning with physical exercise – its example of 'Wake and Shake' can be seen on the Primary Languages website: www.primary languages.org.uk/training_zone/teachers/active_learning/drama/wake_and_shake.aspx.

Here KS2 children are teaching KS1 children 'Savez-vous plantez les choux?' and the video demonstrates the benefits of a physical routine combined with learning the song. The research indicates that 'Learning a co-ordinated series of movements produces increased neurotrophins which stimulate the growth of nerve cells and promotes a greater number of connections between neurons.' In other words, children learn better when both sides of the brain are engaged.

The use of song incorporates the language learning strategies of rhythm, rhyme and repetition, as well as reinforcing vocabulary and language structure (it is probably best to give children some written support when teaching songs). It is a tried and tested method in language learning and there are now many resources to support teachers in teaching songs. As well as the familiar, well-known songs, websites such as www.mamalisa.com have a wealth of material from all over the world. The site has written transcripts and MP3 recordings to download – a wonderful resource for busy teachers.

Learning songs in another language offers opportunities for performance, for example, in weekly assemblies, to other classes, the whole school and also to parents. Learning songs at particular times of year, e.g. Christmas, helps children to gain insight into how other countries celebrate festivals that are familiar to them. I vividly remember one class I had performing a Christmas song: '"Ooh la la, il fait froid," dit le Bonhomme de neige . . .' ('Ooh la la, it's cold,' said the Snowman) at an assembly with very expressive ooh la las, much to the delight of parents and the other children. It stimulated the other children to want to learn the song, so much so that the whole school (KS1 and KS2) learned it and sang it the following week!

'Head and shoulders, knees and toes' is a well-used song to consolidate body-parts vocabulary and can be adapted for use in games, such as 'Jacques a dit'. Adding actions, such as 'Jacques a dit: "Tournez", "Sautez" or "Dansez"' adds interest and can also be used to good effect when it is becoming harder for children to be 'out' – a good tip is for the teacher to do the action of touching the head or dancing: nine times out of ten a child or children will copy the action before realising that the teacher hasn't said 'Jacques a dit'! Unfair, perhaps, but necessary if time is running short in the lesson and there are still 20 children to get 'out'! There are German and Spanish equivalents of 'Head and shoulders' that can be used to similar effect. Extensions of this are games to pin the correct words on a large body drawing once understanding is secure; children can be divided into teams and each given a set of the vocabulary. The first person from a team to reach the drawing with the correct word wins the point.

**Games**, like songs, are a useful way for children to engage with the new language and consolidate understanding. They promote collaborative skills, and most games that children are familiar with adapt very well to language learning. The 'fun' element is an important aspect for foreign language learning in order to sustain motivation, but, as previously mentioned, not at the expense of cognitive development. To this end, games should be planned carefully, with learning objectives, success criteria, a plenary and progression in mind. The following are a few examples of games that can be used:

- Bingo – number calculations can be used instead of single numbers.
- Noughts and crosses – examples of progression were discussed earlier in this chapter.
- Simon says.
- Stepping stones – have a large piece of paper with a river drawn across it and two sets of an appropriate number of stepping stones to get to the other side of the river. This

can also be devised on an IWB. The children are in two teams and must answer questions correctly in order for their team to get to the next stone and cross the river.

- Describing a celebrity. Children in their team's are given envelopes, each with a famous person's name inside it. When the children open their envelopes they must describe their celebrities to the other team, who have to guess the identity, e.g. elle est chanteuse; elle a les cheveux bruns etc. Descriptions and vocabulary can be adapted depending on what needs to be consolidated.
- Weather forecast. Have a pretend television screen (made from a frame from a cardboard box). The children take it in turns to show flashcards or props (e.g. umbrella, sunglasses), as if they are on television. The children have to say the correct weather phrase in the target language. This can be done in pairs, groups or in two teams. Sentences can be built up, e.g. 'Aujourd'hui il pleut.' 'J'ai besoin d'un parapluie.' 'Voici mon parapluie, il est bleu.'

There are a wealth of games that can be used. The QCDA guidance for teachers gives many examples, but it is a good rule of thumb to remember that any favourite and familiar games in English can be adapted, with care, for use in teaching another language.

## Embedding

The discrete teaching of languages and embedding them into the curriculum implies that language learning is part of the whole-school ethos and, as such, can be incorporated into all aspects of school life. It cannot be emphasised enough that the importance of a positive whole-school ethos in relation to language learning is vital for it to be sustainable. Children are very quick to spot negativity and a weak link.

Well-tried examples of a positive whole-school approach are each class taking the register in a different language, greetings round the school, asking common questions in class in the target language, e.g. 'Je peux aller aux toilettes?' [Can I go to the toilets?]; 'Je peux aiguiser mon crayon s'il vous plait?' [Can I sharpen my pencil please?]; 'Puis-je changer mon livre de lecture s'il vous plait?' [Can I change my reading book please?]

In addition:

- practising numbers when lining up;
- daily physical activity;
- performance of language learning in assembly;
- practising weather phrases;
- practising the day and date;
- daily online picture (www.coloriage.com/).

give children an opportunity to practise independently and actively encourage them to do so. Having vocabulary displayed throughout the school also helps to raise the profile of languages and consolidates children's learning.

The Primary Languages Co-ordinator is central to the profile of languages in the school but he/she also needs the support of the head and staff. Linking classes with other countries and ensuring that staff are supported with training and resources in order to develop confidence are all vital to promoting a positive ethos and a successful language learning environment.

## Content Language Integrated Learning

Content Language Integrated Learning (CLIL) means that part or all of the entire curriculum is delivered in the target language. In order for this type of embedding to be successful, careful planning is needed, and also a high degree of confidence and linguistic competence on the teacher's part.

An interesting film clip to watch in relation to Science being approached as CLIL is one funded by the TDA, which can be found on the Universities' Council for the Education of Teachers website: www.ucet.ac.uk/2562.

The following is a possible teaching sequence for Year 4/5 children looking at Impressionism in **Art and Design.** The artist is Monet, and the picture is *Regatta d'Argenteuil.* It is assumed that the children already have an understanding of the Impressionist style of painting and can identify specific features and artists. For each question the children would need to look at the painting. New vocabulary would depend, obviously, on the existing prior knowledge of the children.

### I. Qui est l'artiste?

L'artiste est Claude Monet

### 2. Quelles couleurs voyez-vous dans la peinture?

Je vois:

- ❑   Les bleus, foncés et clairs
- ❑   Turquoise
- ❑   Crème
- ❑   Les verts
- ❑   Ocre brun
- ❑   Brun
- ❑   Rouge
- ❑   Blanc

### 3. Qu'est-ce que vous voyez?

Je vois:

- ❑   La mer
- ❑   Les reflets dans l'eau
- ❑   Les yachts
- ❑   Le ciel
- ❑   Des personnes sur les yachts
- ❑   Les bâtiments
- ❑   Des personnes au bord de la mer
- ❑   L'herbe
- ❑   Autre chose?

**4. Que remarquez-vous sur le style de peinture?**

❏   Ce n'est pas exacte
❏   Un moment d'émotion
❏   Les couleurs brisées
❏   Beaucoup de couleurs
❏   Les impressionnistes

**5. On va peindre!**

•   Essayez de peindre dans le style de Monet *La Regatta d'Argenteuil*
•   Faites d'abord une esquisse ou un dessin en crayon
•   Vous faites les coups de pinceau comme ça . . .
•   Vous avez le papier, les peints, les brosses et de l'eau – allez-y!

When teaching this sequence, teachers would need to consider the following:

•   What vocabulary would you need in order to help the children improve their paintings?
•   What would you emphasise in order for them to achieve their best work?
•   What questions are the children likely to ask?
•   Praise language.
•   Questions to assess understanding both of the task and of the language concepts.

This activity can be extended by giving children the opportunity to visit the website of the Musée d'Orsay, which houses the paintings of many Impressionists and which has resources for primary teachers and an opportunity to make virtual tours of different artists' works. There is a specific site for primary schools that provides resources and detailed information about different artists: www.musee-orsay.fr/en/espace-professionnels/profes sionals/teachers-and-youth-leaders/teaching-resources/online-resources.html.

Of course, the best approach is to take the children to Paris to see the paintings for real!

## Reflection/task

•   Consider a lesson that you have taught that could be suitable for integrating into language learning.

# Chapter 5

# Teaching assistants

This short chapter will consider the role of teaching assistants in the classroom and in the delivery of Primary Languages.

## Working with teaching assistants

There has been a significant growth in the number of teaching assistants deployed in schools, rising from 48,000 in 1997 to 153,000 in 2008, and although recent research has questioned the validity of such a large increase in terms of whether children's progress has improved (Blatchford *et al.* 2004), most teachers have welcomed the increase. The availability of funding for more teaching assistants in primary schools has been beneficial for the busy and overstretched primary teacher. Having another 'body' in the classroom to help small groups of children, deliver additional support programmes or one-to-one support, as well as to help with administrative and classroom tasks, can be invaluable. In initial teacher education great emphasis is placed on instructing trainees to value their teaching assistants through appropriate planning and discussion – which is only right and proper.

The issues surrounding teaching assistants in the classroom are complex and research is throwing up issues such as:

- Does the number of teaching assistants in classrooms now indicate that teachers are less able to teach unaided?
- Are children being educated by a less qualified workforce?
- Are teachers benefiting from teaching assistant support by, for example, having a reduced workload?
- Are teaching assistants being employed and deployed effectively?

In recent years it seems that teaching assistants have been asked to do things that could be construed as being outside their remit – the advent of PPA time, although warmly welcomed by teachers, left many schools with the dilemma of how to cover the 10 per cent remission from teaching that every full-time teacher is now entitled to take out of their teaching week. Supply cover or the appointment of a 'floating teacher' are expensive options; a teacher in a specialist subject teaches that subject to all classes, and this will necessitate supply cover for their own class. Cue teaching assistants, who could cover areas of the curriculum that are perhaps deemed to be of less importance or that teachers like least or with which they feel least confident. RE is one subject area that has fallen foul of this strategy adopted by schools, and it seems that languages is likely to be another. I have lost count of the number of trainees who have told me that languages are covered by a teaching assistant during the teacher's PPA time. This is not to denigrate teaching assistants, but they cannot replace teachers and are not trained to do so. It should be added that teaching assistants' pay does not reflect this and other responsibilities that are placed on them. These are contentious issues, however, and here is not the place to debate them. It is important to note that all teaching assistants and higher level teaching assistants (HLTAs) work under the direction of the class teacher even if the class teacher is not present in the classroom.

For teachers and teaching assistants to work well together, the teaching assistant needs to be aware of planning and assessment and, through discussion, to be able to give an opinion as to how teaching should progress. As such, good working relationships are vital.

## Teaching assistants and Primary Languages

As well as the question of subject knowledge, a good attitude to language learning is pertinent here. If a school has taken the route of having teaching assistants cover for Primary Languages teachers in PPA time, it is essential that they receive training in the delivery of Primary Languages and are supported by the Primary Languages subject leader, and also that positive messages are given to children whilst learning. It may be that the teaching assistant lacks confidence in his or her language learning ability, but an approach of 'learning together' will do much to encourage children's learning.

To help address the need for training the primary workforce the Upskilling Specification has been developed, which is aimed at 'Primary teachers or teaching assistants who have made a beginning in teaching a language, and who now wish to be able to teach with confidence over the 4 years of the primary languages curriculum. This addresses a major need of the primary workforce in the coming period' (CILT Primary Languages website). Its aims are:

- To help teachers gain confidence in using (and improving their use of) the target language in the classroom, enabling them to be more independent and experimental in using the language. This will in turn help their pupils learn and become confident with the language.
- To strengthen links to the Oracy and Literacy strands of the KS2 Framework by cross-referencing language content with skills and activities.
- To reinforce teachers' understanding of language structures and of language learning strategies and, through its indicative content, to support their grasp of intercultural understanding.

The CILT runs pedagogical courses for teaching assistants and HLTAs, as well as upskilling sessions. The TDA has developed (along with other agencies) primary CPD materials aimed at teachers wishing to develop their expertise in teaching Primary Languages. These materials are also suitable for those supporting teachers; they can be downloaded free of charge and are available for French, Spanish and German and can be accessed at: www. primarylanguages.org.uk/professional_development/training_materials__resources/dcsf_ and_tda_materials.aspx. Teaching assistants or HLTAs should have access to the KS2 Framework for Languages in order to support their delivery of the subject.

There are courses available for download from this site that are specifically for teaching assistants and HLTAs and that are produced by the Department for Education as part of the National Languages Strategy. 'This envisages teaching assistants, including native speakers from local communities, playing an important role in the delivery of primary languages' (CILT Primary Languages website).

It is important that teaching assistants are familiar with the rationale for teaching languages in primary schools in that it should be a preparation for a firm basis in learning languages and that it supports oracy and literacy. Schools should aim to provide children with the tools to acquire and develop language skills not just during their schooling but throughout life.

Not all schools will ask their teaching assistants to cover the Primary Languages session during PPA time, but they will require their support in embedding the language as part of a whole-school ethos of language learning, as well as during discrete sessions. Registration, for example, is an area where teaching assistants can contribute very successfully. As mentioned in Chapter 4, embedding through encouraging children to ask everyday questions in the target language is another area where teaching assistants can support language learning. In discrete sessions, the class teacher and teaching assistant can engage in conversation in the target language in order to model role play to children. The teaching assistant is important for giving extra support for children either during a Primary Languages session or afterwards if the teacher's and/or teaching assistant's assessment indicates that some children have not understood the lesson's learning objectives. Clearly, the teaching assistant's awareness of the expectations of the class teacher in all these aspects is vital.

Schools use different models for the organisation of teaching assistants and this is a matter that will need to be considered in terms of language support. Some teaching assistants are allocated to work alongside one or two children and will remain in the same class for the week. Or it may be that the teaching assistants move round the school and will be in different classes and year groups, possibly throughout the day. If this is the case, teaching assistants will be working with both LKS2 and UKS2, where the expectations for linguistic achievement will be very different. Implications for training are vital here, as the teaching assistant will need to be aware of both Upper and Lower KS2 learning objectives and also, where, possible, will be expected to have subject knowledge for both Key Stages.

Cremin *et al.* (2005) looked at three different models for teaching assistant classroom support:

- reflective teamwork (teachers and teaching assistants plan and thoroughly discuss together the ways in which they will advance as a team)
- room management (identifying and dividing teaching tasks; allocating specific roles and activities to people working in the classroom)
- zoning ('a model for allocating roles of those working in the classroom to the classroom geography and the groups that exist therein').

The schools using these strategies adapted them for their own use, with different degrees of success. In relation to Primary Languages, my feeling is that the three models would need to be combined for successful Primary Languages learning to take place when teachers and teaching assistants are working together. Teachers and teaching assistants need to work as a team; the teacher should allocate specific roles to the teaching assistant – for example, assisting with visual aids such as flashcards or props. Zoning is helpful when specific children need, say, help with pronunciation, or to have further visual support.

It is important that head teachers and Primary Languages co-ordinators are aware of the teaching assistants' skills and allocate their expertise appropriately. If a teaching assistant has qualifications in or a working knowledge of the language being taught in the school, it would make sense for that teaching assistant to be allocated to support Primary Languages teaching. This is not to say, however, that no other teaching assistants should be involved, but a balance must be struck, allowing for teaching assistants to use any specific expertise that they have, whilst at the same time offering opportunities for other teaching assistants to add to their professional development and training. Opportunities for teaching assistants and teachers to plan together should be prioritised, in order for a joint approach to teaching and learning to be forged.

## Teaching assistants for EAL learners and Primary Languages

Research (Cummins 1981, Collier and Thomas 1989) indicates that it takes as long as seven years for pupils learning English as an additional language (EAL) to acquire a level of English proficiency comparable to that of their native English-speaking peers. Teachers clearly cannot wait for EAL pupils to develop this high level of English-language proficiency before tackling the demands of the curriculum.

'EAL children will become confused if they have to learn another language as well as English' is a statement frequently voiced in one form or another, a concept that is discussed further in Chapters 6 and 8.

Learning a language is not a solitary process: it is necessary to engage with another speaker or speakers in order to learn and progress. EAL children are practised in transferring linguistic and cognitive skills, and teaching assistants can make use of these skills to support their Primary Languages learning. Rather than thinking that learning another language may be more difficult for EAL children, it is more helpful to ask: What knowledge and skills do children who have English as an additional language bring to the Primary Languages classroom? How can we extend these skills? The class teacher can then approach planning so as to enable teaching assistants to support EAL children in the best way possible, taking into account the three principles of the National Curriculum's statutory inclusion statement, in which the teaching assistant has a vital role to play:

(a)  Setting suitable learning challenges
(b)  Responding to the diverse needs of pupils
(c)  Overcoming potential barriers to learning and assessment for individuals and groups of children.

It is not always helpful for EAL children to have only teaching assistant support. Grouping less advanced EAL children with more advanced EAL learners (in terms of linguistic competence) can be very beneficial.

## Reflection

- How would you support a teaching assistant whose approach to the delivery of Primary Languages is either negative or lacking in confidence?
- Do you feel that teaching assistant support in Primary Languages is different to other subject support? If so, how?
- Do you feel that teaching assistants are best deployed in supporting lower-ability children in the delivery of Primary Languages?

# Chapter 6

# Intercultural understanding

This chapter considers:

- a definition of intercultural understanding;
- implications and ideas for planning to include intercultural understanding in the curriculum;
- partner schools;
- taking children abroad;
- community languages and English as an additional language (EAL).

## What is intercultural understanding?

Intercultural understanding is one of the three main strands of the KS2 Framework for Languages and is rightly given equal status with oracy and literacy, which are the 'nuts and bolts' of learning a language.

When Socrates was asked where he came from, according to Cicero, he said that he was 'a citizen of the world'. A more recent quotation from an international newspaper editor perhaps sums up what our view of the world should be as global citizens:

> The most important thing that schools can do is to make people aware that understanding the world is very much part of the requirement of being an educated person. There should be some shame attached to not being more aware of the world, not having some mastery of foreign language.
>
> (Fareed Zakaria, *Newsweek International*, 26 December 2005)

The view of one academic is that of Professor Noam Chomsky, Professor of Linguistics at Massachusetts Institute of Technology:

> Language embodies the world view of a culture and is unique to the culture that created it. It reflects values and concepts that are deemed to be the most important by a culture. A language describes the culture it comes from.
>
> (Chomsky, 1965)

Learning another language enables the learner to step inside the psyche of another culture. It is only learning a language that enables us to do this. If we cannot communicate within the culture, we cannot access it. We cannot participate fully in the customs and practices that occur across all societies yet are, at the same time, unique to each one because of each society's different social and verbal interactions. Without knowledge of the language it is harder to discern sensitive aspects in exchanges with other people, and misunderstandings as well as mistrust can develop. Today, in a world that is ever more interdependent, it is more important than ever that children are aware of other cultures.

> Intercultural understanding begins with individuals who have language abilities and who can provide one's own nation or community with an insider's view into foreign cultures, who can understand foreign news sources, and give insights into other perspectives on international situations and current events. For survival in the global community, every nation needs such individuals. A person proficient in other languages can bridge the gap between cultures, contribute to international diplomacy, promote national security and world peace, and successfully engage in international trade.
>
> (Vistawide, 'World Languages and Culture')

All children should be given the opportunity to become such individuals, and gaining competence in one or more languages alongside studying and engaging in the cultures of those countries will help to achieve this.

Language learning should promote intercultural understanding by arousing curiosity about other cultures. It should also deepen awareness and appreciation of one's own culture.

## Implications and ideas for planning

Intercultural understanding can be approached and included in many areas of the curriculum, and technology now affords direct opportunities for children to engage with children from other countries through video-conferencing, via Skype telephone calls and via e-mail.

In Chapter 4 we looked at how planning and implementing language learning can be embedded into the curriculum. Intercultural understanding can be approached in a similar way by considering how different curriculum areas can offer opportunities for children to understand a different culture and way of life.

This can be achieved at very simple levels when the language is first introduced. For example, teaching children how to greet each other in another language immediately demonstrates cultural differences. The French shake hands and/or kiss each other on both cheeks (up to four times!), which British people do not do. (It is true to say that as a nation the British are a lot more 'huggy' than they used to be, but shaking of hands tends to be for first meetings of adults and does not happen when people meet each other on a regular basis.) Asking the children to move around the classroom and greet each other in French and with shaking of hands (kissing on the cheek is perhaps harder to implement!) is effective and an activity that they will remember for both its linguistic and its cultural content.

As children progress through the curriculum units (if schools are using the QCDA guidance, for example), other opportunities arise. In Unit 2, for example, which focuses on learning songs, it is quite possible to find translations of English songs that children will be familiar with, but it is so much better to find authentic French songs that they can learn. Look at www.mamalisa.com, which is an excellent website that has literally hundreds of authentic songs, plus translations and MP3 recordings from all over the world. Thus, instead of using the translation of 'The Farmer's in his Den', children can learn and sing 'Meunier, tu dors', a well-loved French song. The children can be told that it's one of the first songs that is sung to a baby, and can be taught the traditional and well-known hand movements that accompany it. Thus, the children develop an understanding of nursery rhyme equivalents in other countries. Comparable UK songs are 'Incy Wincy Spider' and 'Round and Round the Garden'. The QCDA schemes of work give much good and helpful advice to enable children to progress and it is likely that schools will use them for a good while, until they feel confident to 'break out', as with other QCDA schemes of work, and include other facets.

Looking at the different areas of the curriculum may help to start thinking about different opportunities.

In Unit 9 of the QCDA schemes of work (L'Histoire) **Literacy** is the obvious link, and it is true to say that when children are familiar with stories in English they will be able to gather the gist if a story is told to them (with visual clues) in another language. Examples of 'The Sleeping Beauty' and 'Jack and the Beanstalk' are included. 'The Sleeping Beauty' is, in fact, of French origin ('La Belle au Bois dormant', written by Charles Perrault in 1697) and was later adapted by the German Brothers Grimm; but the story is so entrenched in our own story-telling culture that children are unlikely to know this, and it provides a wonderful opportunity to deepen children's intercultural understanding of the origins of fairy tales.

This approach to intercultural understanding can be extended if, for example, stories are chosen that are French in origin but familiar to British children. Why not, choose 'Babar the Elephant', which offers an opportunity to gain some insight into French culture as Babar flees to Paris. *Le Petit Prince* by Antoine de Saint-Exupéry, one of the best-selling books ever, would be a challenging and interesting book for Year 6 children to read. It is a deeply philosophical book which would help children to gain an insight into the rich philosophical legacy of France (Voltaire, Descartes, de Beauvoir, Sartre, Pascal, Rousseau, to name but a few). From this, children could be introduced to some well-known philosophical statements such as: 'Je pense, donc je suis' (Descartes, 'I think therefore I am'). Many schools have begun to teach thinking skills through philosophical discussion, an approach that can begin at the Foundation Stage and that is 'an educational approach aimed at learning through asking more and better questions and through co-operative dialogue in a community of enquiry' (Philosophy for Children, P4C, www.philosophyineducation.com/index.html).

*Don Quixote* by Miguel de Cervantes is an obvious Spanish choice that offers many cultural opportunities. The website www.donquijote.org/vmuseum/, which is a virtual Don Quixote museum, has information relating to food, music and art that can easily be adapted for primary age children.

**Religious Education** affords rich opportunities to develop intercultural understanding, but unfortunately teaching of this subject it can be fraught with fear and, as with languages, a lack of confidence. The following may be helpful for those who consider themselves both fearful and lacking in expertise.

### Mardi Gras (literally 'Fat Tuesday')

Cooking pancakes and learning about how other countries celebrate Shrove Tuesday can incorporate a wealth of learning opportunities. Don't just look at French 'crêpes', but consider Spain and the wider world. In Spain and Hispanic countries carnivals are the norm, and cities explode in a riot of colour and celebration. Images and videos of these events can easily be found on the internet and, used on the IWB, can give children insight into how our celebrations may seem a little tame in comparison.

The Mardi Gras celebrations of Venice, known as the Venice Carnival, are home to the real Mardi Gras masks. The mask makers are especially highly regarded and the two-week celebration is famous throughout the world. Making Mardi Gras masks (as well as learning some Italian) lends itself extremely well to embedding languages and intercultural understanding into **Art and Design** as well as **Design and Technology.**

Perhaps contrast this with some of the traditions in the UK, which can help children to develop an appreciation of their own culture and traditions. Scarborough, in North Yorkshire, for example, closes down at midday on Shrove Tuesday and everyone heads to the beach for an afternoon of skipping. This is a tradition that is thought to date back to 'Ball Day' in the later nineteenth century, when everyone had an afternoon off and Scarborough's promenade was lined with stalls selling toys such as tops, balls and skipping ropes. There is also a Pancake Bell, which is always rung by the Deputy Mayor. In 1903 it was recorded that some 'bairns' were seen skipping near the lifeboat, and the day was hailed as a skipping holiday in 1927. Other possible origins of the skipping tradition are that the fishermen would give their old fishing nets to the children so that they could use them for skipping ropes (for more information see www.information-britain.co.uk/customdetail.php?id=37.)

## Easter

In France this is a national holiday that is celebrated by all from a religious perspective, much more so than in the UK. The church bells remain silent from Good Friday until Easter Sunday, when everyone celebrates with the wealth of goodies that are available in the shops.

In Germany there is tradition of huge bonfires on Easter Saturday evenings. The Easter fires are burned to symbolise the end of winter and bad omen. They are a very popular tradition and large numbers of people assemble to enjoy the event. Then, there is the tradition of families having breakfast together on Easter Sunday. Easter baskets full with sweets, eggs and small presents are hidden and the children have to find them. Colourful Easter eggs are decorated with traditional designs and are exchanged amongst friends.

Easter is regarded as the most important festival in Spain. Known as 'Semana Santa' in Spanish, it is an occasion of celebration and merriment. The celebrations start with 'Domingo de Ramos', or Palm Sunday, and finish with 'Lunes de Pascua', or Easter Monday. Easter Day is observed as a religious occasion by the people of Spain, who commemorate the resurrection of Jesus with much fanfare and gaiety. Parades are organised in which people carry huge, leafy palm or olive branches that have been blessed in the church. Along with the religious festivity, in Spain, Easter is also a great time for family get-togethers. On Easter Day a sumptuous feast is prepared in every household and special dishes like 'La Mona' or Easter egg, pork sausage and calçots, hazelnut cream with pheasant ravioli truffles and Italian Easter bread are cooked. The festivity of Eastertide extends to every street, with loud sounds, bright lights, nicely dressed people, and celebration and enjoyment everywhere. Easter is also as a holiday time for the Spanish, and many people rush to the country's historic sites to bask in the glory of the festival.

Again, contrast this with the largely secular approach in the UK, which focuses on Easter eggs and the Easter Bunny tradition.

### Christmas

The traditions of Christmas vary from one country to another and children can be introduced to the Festival of St Nicholas, which is widely celebrated in Europe, and its accompanying traditions. The festival is on 6 December and St Nicholas is the patron saint of children. St Nicolas is very important in Holland, Switzerland and Germany. The Dutch name is Sinterklaas.

At Christmas time in France, children put shoes by the fireplace (contrast with stockings in the UK) in the hope that Père Noel will bring them toys. The main meal is eaten on Christmas Eve (Le Réveillon) and consists of goose, turkey, chicken or beef, a fish dish, cheese, bread, wine and fruit (again, contrast this with UK tradition of Christmas Day lunch). A Bûche de Noel (Yule Log) is served after the meal – something that the children could make. In France there is also a celebration meal on Christmas Day, but there is much greater emphasis on Christmas Eve celebrations. In France everyone goes back to work on 26 December, as the Boxing Day holiday does not exist.

### Boxing Day

It might be useful to look at the origins of the Boxing Day holiday on 26 December, which contrasts with the holidays in other European countries and is also called St Stephen's Day.

Boxing Day is a public holiday that forms part of the Christmas festivities in most of the countries that were once part of the British Empire. It was originally the first working day after Christmas Day, but is now always celebrated on 26 December, regardless of the day of the week on which it falls. Developing children's understanding and appreciation of their own cultural heritage is extended through looking at other countries' cultures and traditions.

### Epiphany

This is an important festival in France but is virtually ignored in the UK. On Epiphany (the first Sunday after 1 January), many families in Provence follow a tradition of eating the Gâteau des Rois – (or Galette des Rois in the northern half of France and Belgium). This is a kind of king cake with a trinket – usually a porcelain or plastic figurine of a king, or a fava bean (la fève) – hidden inside. The lucky person who gets the piece of cake containing the trinket is crowned King (or Queen) for a day. The cakes can be found in most French bakeries during the month of January and are accompanied by a paper crown. The galette consists of flaky puff pastry layers with a dense centre of frangipani (made from or flavoured like almonds), while the provençale gâteau is a crown-shaped brioche with candied fruits (fruits confits).

Giving children the opportunity to learn about this festival will provide an important insight into French culture. Learning the traditional song that children sing ('J'aime la galette') and the movements that accompany it, as well as the children perhaps making the cake (with the trinket inside) will give them further insight. The correct procedure is given below.

> J'aime la galette, *(walk in a circle, holding hands, to the right)*
> Savez-vous comment? *(change directions – go left)*
> Quand elle bien faite *(go right)*
> Avec du beurre dedans. *(go left)*

Trala la la la la la la lère, *(hands over head, walk inwards)*
Tra la la la la la la la la, *(step back out in circle)*
Tra la la la la la la la lère, *(hands over head, walk in)*
Tra la la la la la la la la. *(step back out in circle)*

Cut the galette and give to the children. Instruct them to wait ('Attendez').
Everyone must eat carefully and at the same time. Teach children to say 'Miam Miam'
(yum, yum).
When a child finds the trinket, they must say 'le voici'.
Crown the king or queen.
The children say 'Vive le roi' or 'Vive la reine'.

All of the above are religious festivals and an important part of the culture of countries
that children should know about.

In **History,** when looking at World War II, children could look at how other countries
mark important remembrance ceremonies. They could look at the celebrations in Paris for
Armistice Day, which is a national holiday in France, whereas in the UK it is not. Children
could gain insight into France's different approach to this memorial day, which is due,
amongst other things, to the fact that France was invaded by the Germans, whilst England,
being an island, was not. Contrast this with the (optional) two minutes' silence that is
practised in the UK (although there are remembrance services in churches and an official
service at the Cenotaph in London, in which the Queen and government officials take part).

Culture has many aspects, of course. Music, dance and food are an integral part of any
society, and have been for centuries.

A whole-school approach to developing intercultural understanding of different countries
should be welcomed and encouraged. Figure 6.1 shows the timetable of a European Day
that I held in a school where I taught and that encompassed key elements of intercultural
understanding of some European countries, and also involved all teachers, teaching assistants
and children, as well as kitchen and administrative staff.

This was a very successful day for all concerned and the dancing and music culminated
in a performance for parents and the school at the end of the day, which was very much
enjoyed and appreciated. It was important to have the whole school involved, including,
as mentioned, the kitchen staff, who embraced the whole day with gusto. The food aspect
was a vital part of the day and provided an opportunity to involve parents, who were invited
to the lunch as well as the performances (it proved extremely popular, so much so that
there were two sittings!). In addition, the day involved the wider community – a local dance
school, local restaurants and a local musician. Other ideas that could have been included
were an opera workshop, other restaurants (e.g. Spanish tapas) and art workshops on artists
from European countries.

Days such as these raise the profile of Primary Languages considerably for teachers,
children, parents and the community, especially if the local radio and newspapers are in
formed. Photographs and videos can be posted on the school's website. Opportunities for
follow-up work are considerable; for example, children can learn about the 'Blue Danube'
waltz, which is an opportunity for them to learn about the location of the River Danube.

Intercultural understanding need not necessarily be limited by the languages that the
school is studying. Extending children's knowledge of other countries and at the same time
providing a taster of languages outside their experience is very beneficial. Figure 6.2 shows

| Class | Boules (Approx. 5 sets per class – to be played outside) | Pizza and Italian (Mr. Staiano, in Christine's room) | German (Mrs. Sleightholme, in classrooms) | Dancing (Miss Hatton, Hall, classes 4 and 5, class 6 outside) |
|---|---|---|---|---|
| 8 | 9.30–10.00 | 10.00–10.20 | 10.45–11.15 | |
| 7 | 11.00–11.30 | 10.20–10.45 NB Later break 10.45–11.00 | 9.30–10.00 | |
| 6 | 11.30–12.00 | | 10.00–10.30 | 1.15–2.30 (can-can) |
| 5 | 2.00–2.30 | | 11.15–11.40 | 9.15–10.30 (Irish and Scottish) |
| 4 | 10.00–10.30 NB Later break 10.30–10.45 | | 1.00–1.20 | 10.45–12.00 (Flamenco) |
| 3 | 1.00–1.30 | 10.45–11.05 | 11.45–12.00 | |
| 2 | 10.30–11.00 | 11.10–11.30 | 10.30–10.45 | |
| 1 | 10.30–11.00 | 11.35–11.55 | 1.20–1.30 | |

**Notes from Primary Languages teacher to staff:**

- Everyone will have a French breakfast between 9 and 9.30 which will be served in your classrooms!
- Everyone (except Class 6) to attend a concert by Mr. James of different European music, composers and instruments in the Hall from 1.30 until 2.00
- Everyone to attend dance demonstration by Classes 4, 5 and 6 from 2.30 until 3.00
- Lunch and break times as normal except where indicated (Lunch menu – Strudel (meat option and veg option); boulangère potatoes; julienne carrots and petits pois; Black Forest Gateau)
- I have given everyone ideas for some French activities for each class - if you want more, let me know!

*Figure 6.1* Timetable for a European Day

an information sheet for the teachers of a Cold Climate Day that was held for a whole school.

It can be seen from this information for teachers that the children were studying far more than the languages of those countries. The outdoor survival techniques sessions ranged from instructing children in the use of survival bags and finding out about weather conditions prior to undertaking any kind of walk or expedition, to building an outdoor shelter.

The CILT Primary Languages website provides some helpful video clips of children actively engaging in intercultural understanding in areas such as songs, games and making food.

---

**Cold Climate Day February 9th**

Each teacher will receive a pack this week with the following in order to choose activities for the day:

- Information on Scandinavian capital cities and pictures
- Recipes to make simple Swedish biscuits and cold food (e.g. Danish open sandwiches); also rye bread recipe
- Instructions on how to teach some basic phrases in Swedish and Norwegian
- Geographical features of Norway (fjords) and Sweden (forestry). Effects of glaciers
- Samples of Scandinavian and Icelandic artists' work and suggestions (e.g. Munch – *The Scream*)
- Scandinavian flags
- Suggestions for music to listen to
- Information on Hans Christian Andersen/the story of the Little Mermaid and suggestions for follow-up work
- Information on climate (e.g. Denmark – temperate)
- Information and activity suggestions related to Shackleton and South Pole
- Snowboarding DVD
- DVD about North Pole expedition
- Each class will have a session with Simon from East Barnby on **outdoor survival techniques**. Timetables are in teachers' packs
- Each class will have a visit from McCain's for some information/activities about freezing

In addition there is the meal at lunchtime (soup and rye bread, Danish meatballs and apple cake – yum yum) and the ice-skating booked for Monday 6th March which will be from 3 pm to 8 pm.

---

*Figure 6.2* Teachers' information sheet for Cold Climate Day

## Partner schools – a rich resource

Having a partner school in another country is not a new approach in schools, but considering partner schools in terms of developing our children's linguistic capabilities is somewhat newer.

Schools find partners in other countries through a variety of means – perhaps through personal links or through actively searching on websites such as the Global Gateway (www.globalgateway.org/), which provides support for schools wishing to link with other schools all over the world. There are opportunities to partner with schools in other continents, and the British Council offers funding for 'Small groups of schools from the UK partner with schools usually from two different countries within one continent. The participating regions include sub-Saharan Africa, North Africa, Central and South Asia, East Asia, Middle East, China and Latin America.'

Reciprocal funding is currently also available from the British Council for schools to visit each other, and this contributes enormously to children's intercultural understanding. I had an opportunity to visit India with a partner school I worked with and the Indian teachers came to visit us. For that particular school, the learning was extremely beneficial because it otherwise had very few multicultural opportunities, being a small rural school. Such exchanges and experiences also offer considerable opportunities for follow-up work, for example, dance workshops, art activities (e.g. India: Mendhi patterns, Rangoli patterns), food preparation and tasting, music and stories. Activities such as these offer extensive opportunities to draw on the expertise of local communities, which affords further possibilities to develop intercultural understanding.

Partnering with schools in South America and Africa, for example, presents schools that are studying, say, Spanish or French with further opportunities to develop both language competence and intercultural understanding outside of Europe, which will demonstrate to children just how far-reaching language learning can be, both logistically and cerebrally. Such opportunities as are available should be exploited to their full extent so as to enable teachers and children to maximise their teaching and learning.

One way of doing this is through schools exchanging information and techniques on a curriculum theme. One school that was partnered with an African school looked at art and artists in both countries and children from Foundation Stage to Year 6 participated. The children looked at how artists used different media, different subject matter and different techniques, and applied this to their own creations. Information and examples were exchanged in order for the children to see at first hand the differences and similarities in techniques. The event culminated in an exhibition of art from both countries, for both parents and the wider community. The teachers involved in this project were very excited at the potential of learning in this way. As Jones and Coffey (2006) state: 'Teachers who are motivated by the experience of their own learning are likely to excite their pupils in turn.' If primary teachers can succeed in motivating children to learn languages, and that motivation is sustained, then children in the UK will be in a far better position to learn languages at secondary level and the hitherto indifferent approach to language learning could become a thing of the past.

Communication with partner schools can take place via a regular weekly e-mail message or through a weekly video-conferencing session. This is much more achievable and more likely to last than is children writing lengthy letters to their counterparts on a less regular basis, and is also more meaningful for them. The whole class can discuss the responses and children can take it in turns to compose and send the e-mails or take part in the video conference. Communication can take place in both languages in order for both schools to develop linguistic competence. This approach can be varied through discussion. It may be that the schools decide to write and speak to each other in their native tongue for part of the time, in order for the children to see the correct model, but having the opportunity to talk to each other in the target languages is a wonderful prospect that should not be passed over. Again, this can be a whole-school initiative so that each class is corresponding with the partner school. Some schools do this and culminate Year 6 with a visit to the country so that the children can meet their counterparts. If children know that this is likely to happen and is on the school agenda, it provides a great incentive for them to keep in touch.

It is a good idea for schools and their partners to develop an understanding of their different educational systems and approaches. This can be achieved by, for example, each school planning to deliver a particular topic at the same time and exchange information so that the children can see how children learn in other countries and cultures.

## Taking primary children on trips abroad

Our present culture screams 'no' to anything that might put children at risk, which is nothing short of a tragedy. The risk assessment, health and safety and planning procedures involved have conspired to deter teachers from taking children on trips in the UK, let alone to Europe.

However, nothing develops children's intercultural understanding more than participating in a trip abroad. This might sound like a scary prospect for teachers, but, having taken primary children to France several times, some as young as 8, I can confidently say that the experiences gained by them far outweighed any scary thoughts or moments I might have had both in planning and leading the trips.

### Why should we take children on a trip abroad?

The reasons for taking children on school trips abroad are:

- Primary Languages entitlement in KS2;
- enhancement of intercultural understanding;
- developing speaking/listening skills in the target language;
- extending phonological awareness and understanding;
- giving real meaning to language learning, making it relevant;
- motivating language learning;
- broadening horizons, gaining independence, experiencing being away from home;
- outdoor/adventurous opportunities (there are now many centres in Europe that offer these experience for primary children from other countries).

Despite some initial concern on the part of some parents, one school recently took children on a very successful trip to France. The school was supported by the local authority and it was felt not only that the trip would benefit the children, but also that the teaching of languages would be seen in a more favourable light. Preparations and planning were meticulous and included a reconnaissance trip made by the teachers to ensure that they would be absolutely certain of the standards that they could tell the parents and children to expect and to decide on the itinerary in detail after having experienced it themselves.

The itinerary that was planned is shown in Figure 6.3.

The trip took place over five days and the teachers sent pictures back regularly to be uploaded to the school's website so that the parents could see the children on the different stages of the journey to France and during the trip itself. The parents were then able to see that the children were safe and enjoying themselves. The trip was hugely successful and had a tremendously positive impact on the school as a whole. When I spoke to some of the children on their return, I asked them what they felt had been the best part of the experience. It was extremely gratifying to hear children say that, for them, the best part had been being able to understand what French people were saying to them. They had been thrilled that when they visited a goat farm, they could ask questions in French and understand what the farmer was saying to them. From that experience, they understood immediately how important it is to learn a language, in terms of relevance and in order to gain understanding of the culture. They also said that France 'felt different', and when they were probed further on this point they discussed a great variety of aspects of the country that had struck them.

- 'The electricity pylons were a different shape and so the landscape didn't look the same as ours.'
- 'The irrigation is different so the countryside looked different.' (This from a farmer's son!)

## Our itinerary

| | | Morning | Afternoon | | | Evening |
|---|---|---|---|---|---|---|
| **Mon** | B r e a k f a s t | 4 am Departure | | | E v e n i n g   M e a l | Scavenger Hunt |
| **Tues** | | Étaples Market Language Tasks Crêpes tasting | Zip Wire | Raft Building | | Château Olympics |
| **Wed** | | Château Tour Rue town exploration | Archery | Abseiling | | Night walk/Blind Trail |
| **Thurs** | | Goat Farm Visit Chocolate Factory Demonstration | Initiative Challenges | Assault Course | | Social Evening |
| **Fri** | | Return Journey | | | | 8 pm |

*Figure 6.3* Itinerary for a school trip to France

- 'All the houses had shutters.'
- 'The bread shops sold different things and the cakes were prettier.'
- 'There were different smells.'
- 'The motorways weren't so crowded and you had to pay.'

The teachers also commented that motivation in language learning sessions increased markedly, and that it was possible to identify those children who had been on the trip and those who had not, with particular reference to their pronunciation: children who had participated had much better accents than those who hadn't. The trip was a resounding success and is to be set firmly on the school's agenda for children in Years 5 and 6 on a biennial basis.

The teachers summed up the outcomes of the trip as shown in Figure 6.4. The teacher involved commented: 'Initially I was worried that the responsibility would be too great to take children abroad, but once there it was no different to the responsibility I feel in taking children somewhere in the UK.' This should encourage other teachers to consider a European trip.

Finally, the benefits of this trip were praised by a local authority representative who accompanied the group and who stated in his report: 'In conclusion, this was a particularly well-organised and managed experience which has brought knowledge, understanding and experience to these young people *which can only be achieved through these means.*'

Planning, of course, is the key to any successful residential trip. When preparing to take children abroad it may be helpful to use the checklist in Figure 6.5.

## Outcomes

- Whetted appetite for language learning
  - Insight into another culture
    - Increased self-confidence
      - Independence
        - New experiences/challenges
          - Acquisition of new skills

*Figure 6.4* Outcomes of school trip to France

### Teachers and trainees going abroad

As well as children participating in trips abroad, it is important that teachers and trainees are encouraged to take advantage of the many opportunities there are now to travel to other countries, both as part of their professional development and in order to develop their own intercultural understanding.

Many initial teacher training providers offer trainees a 4-week school experience in a school in Europe, which is currently funded by the TDA. Trainees who have taken this opportunity return with a deeply enriched understanding of the country's culture and education system, as well as greatly improved linguistic competence. This kind of experience demands a relatively good grasp of the language of the country being visited, but many trainees who wish to develop their linguistic skills perhaps do not have sufficient command of the language to undertake any teaching. Some providers offer shorter residential visits (usually funded by the trainee) that aim for an 'immersion' approach, but without the demands of teaching, so that the participant can concentrate on developing language competence. An example of this type of approach is a visit offered by one university, in which trainees participate in a 'setting other than schools' placement. This could be in a museum or in some other setting where children visit, and enables trainees to engage with children and at the same time develop linguistic competence. This type of placement is proving very popular in my own institution as trainees become more aware of the need to develop their language skills and realise that it makes them more 'marketable' in terms of job prospects.

For qualified teachers, the Primary Teachers Project offered by the British Council is an exciting project that enables teachers to spend two weeks in France, Germany or Spain. The first week is devoted to intensive language and methodology training, while the second is spent work-shadowing in a primary school. Information relating to this can be found at www.primarylanguages.org.uk/professional_development/cilt_events/primary_teachers_pr oject.aspx. A contribution towards supply cover is available for this project, which, it is hoped, will encourage heads and teachers to take part.

| Trip abroad checklist | |
|---|---|
| Plan optimum time for visit and choose destination | |
| Contact local authority to ensure they are supportive and to make sure that any administrative requirements are fulfilled | |
| Preliminary questionnaire to parents asking indication of commitment to ascertain numbers | |
| When destination is decided, plan a reconnaissance trip to take into account:<br>• Length of journey<br>• Logistics for any visits made<br>• Activities to develop language competence (e.g. buying stamps, visits to restaurants/cafés)<br>• Activities/visits to develop intercultural understanding<br>• Equipment provided so children can be told what they need to bring<br>• Learning outcomes<br>• Health and safety/risk assessment<br>• SEN/inclusion considerations<br>Costings to include:<br>• Transport (UK and destination country)<br>• Accommodation (full board is best – many centres provide packed lunches for day trips)<br>• Activity costs<br>• Sundries<br>• Funding for low-income families | |
| After booking made, second information letter and consent form to parents to include destination, details of costs, timings | |
| Adults to accompany trip (teachers and teaching assistants) | |
| Apply for collective passport (far easier than each child taking/applying for their own) | |
| Detailed letter to parents reiterating previous information and also advice concerning timings/travel/equipment/clothes/money/contact details/Insurance requirements (EHIC – European Health Insurance Card, apply online: https://www.ehic.org.uk/Internet/home.do | |
| Identify resources needed | |
| Prepare booklet/journal for children to record and reflect | |
| Cameras, video recorders etc. | |
| Consider an item of clothing which all wear to make it easy to identify children should they wander off slightly from the group (e.g. brightly coloured baseball caps, fluorescent jerkins etc.) | |
| Consideration of follow-up activities to trip | |

*Figure 6.5* Checklist for a school trip abroad

## Community languages and EAL

> Community languages are languages spoken by members of minority groups or
> communities within a majority language context.
>
> (National Association for Language Development
> in the Curriculum [NALDIC])

More and more children are entering primary school with varying degrees of proficiency in another language, and often more than one. Nearly 15 per cent of children are known to have a language other than English as their first language. Strategies for and discussion of teaching Primary Languages to EAL children are developed further in Chapter 8.

It is not known exactly how many languages are in spoken in the UK – some will have been used for perhaps hundreds of years, others only relatively recently. NALDIC states: 'a recent survey carried out in London has identified some 307 languages, 20 of which have over 2000 speakers.'

Many minority communities provide complementary schooling in the mother tongue of their community, and successive governments have encouraged such schooling, deeming minority communities to be responsible for maintaining their cultural and linguistic heritage.

The promotion and development of minority community languages within schools enables them to reach out to their minority communities and helps to acknowledge the importance of prior knowledge brought to language learning by bilingual pupils. The presence of EAL children offers a rich resource for further developing children's intercultural understanding, and some schools are teaching a minority community language within the curriculum, which offers children an added dimension. One school in Bradford, for example, teaches Arabic to the children one afternoon a week, using a cross-curricular approach to take into account music, poetry, festivals and food.

The NALDIC website provides many references and ideas for teachers to incorporate community languages in the curriculum, thus giving children the opportunity for using their mother tongue beyond the home: www.naldic.org.uk/ITTSEAL2/teaching/Using communitylanguagesinthemainstreamclassroom.cfm.

Bhatt *et al.* (2004) suggest the following checklist:

- Find out what complementary schools are in your local area and make contact with them. Your local education authority may keep a list; the library may advertise; bilingual/EAL teachers, parents and children will know of some.
- Invite complementary school teachers and administrators to any open days at the school.
- Offer to attend complementary schools' prize giving events where the schools share students. Show commitment to their bilingual and multicultural projects.
- Use mainstream school buildings to house complementary school classes.
- If a complementary school uses the mainstream school site, provide permanent space for materials storage, equipment, section of the library, a notice board.
- Use the mainstream classroom to reflect the home and community languages of the children studying there. Make the mainstream classroom a multilingual space.
- Put up a community/language/culture notice board giving information about bilingual, community and multicultural events.
- Find out if your teachers work in other complementary school settings – ask them to do professional development workshops for other teachers in the school.

- Engage bilingual parents in multilingual homework activities – not just for early bilingual learners until they learn English.
- Find out phrases in different languages which highlight respect and good citizenship and positive attitudes to learning: display these on notice boards around the school.
- Ask a head teacher of a complementary school to give an assembly.
- Encourage other bilingual teachers, parents and assistants to actively promote bilingual interactions in classrooms for learning beyond a transition to English.
- Encourage small-scale research and/or practical projects which would harness the potential links between complementary and mainstream schooling.
- Incorporate teaching and learning experiences of complementary schooling into individual pupil profiles.
- Work with complementary schools to facilitate registration for examinations in community languages.

In addition, Blackledge (1998) recommends the following:

- **Make languages visible**. Many schools have taken a first step towards incorporating pupils' home and community languages into the learning environment by providing signs and notices in the languages of the community. Welcome signs in several languages give a clear and immediate signal to all visitors; labels on displays in the main languages and scripts of the pupils give status to the languages. These labels and notices should be checked: make sure that a notice in an Asian language is not hung upside-down!
- **Provide dual-language texts.** When choosing books for the classroom, look for texts written in English and the community languages of the pupils. These should not only be stories which originate in the pupils' culture but also texts which reflect the pupils' lives in England. Although many young children will not yet be biliterate, they can take home dual-text books and read with their parents, who may be literate in their community language, but not in English. The presence of the community language in the children's reading book affirms their cultural and linguistic identity.
- **Provide opportunities for pupils to write in their home/community language.** Pupils will respond to the task of writing in their home/community language when they feel that they have the respect and trust of the teacher. Appropriate tasks for development of biliteracy include writing and publishing dual-language texts for young children, writing articles for the school newspaper, writing letters to the home country, writing dual-language assemblies for performance, and writing home-culture stories.
- **Language as curriculum content.** Languages can be valued and affirmed when teachers place them at the heart of pupils' learning. This may be by talking and writing about languages in the primary school (e.g. 'I speak to my sister in English, I speak to my mother in Sylheti . . .'), or, more formally, by studying community languages (e.g. Urdu) for examinations in the secondary school.
- **Involve minority parents in their children's learning.** One of the most important areas for developing parental input in young children's learning is in the teaching of reading. It is the responsibility of the school to ensure that all parents feel confident about supporting their children's reading, even when they do not read, write or speak English. Teachers need to speak to parents about their role in talking about text in home languages, asking appropriate questions, and building on existing literacy practices.

It is important for children to know that their own language and culture are valued. When looking at celebrations, ensure that important dates from the ethnic backgrounds of all children are discussed and studied at appropriate times of the year. Thus, it is important for teachers to be aware when important celebrations take place for children in their class. It is a good idea to have these celebrations marked on a class calendar that all the children can see. Displays are a useful way of respecting different celebrations, as is role play.

Ask children to bring in their favourite stories in their own language. Asking children to give a synopsis of their preferred books can greatly help their language development in English. Children whose mother tongue is English can also gain much from this kind of activity. Considering and learning about other cultures helps children to reflect upon and appreciate their own cultural identity. Thus, language and culture can and should be taught in an integrated way.

The CILT sums up intercultural understanding for primary children as follows:

> Developing intercultural understanding in primary schools adds a valuable dimension to language learning and to the primary curriculum. Opportunities are created to arouse children's curiosity and help them become aware of similarities and differences between people and their daily lives. Despite its complexity, intercultural understanding can begin to be developed in primary schools as long as we make sure the tasks are linked to the world of the child.
>
> (CILT Primary Languages website)

## Reflection

The notion of intercultural competence is defined by Meyer (1991) as 'the ability of a person to behave adequately in a flexible manner when confronted with actions, attitudes and expectations of representatives of foreign cultures'.

- Do you feel that integrating intercultural understanding with the teaching of languages is one way to achieve this? How else can teachers and children develop intercultural competence?
- Consider your own skills and talents. How could you use them to develop intercultural understanding within the school?
- Now consider people whom you know within your community. Are there any people who could support any intercultural initiatives that you might want to introduce?
- Begin to think about where you could take children on a trip abroad.

# Chapter 7

# Assessing Primary Languages

This chapter considers:

- Assessment for learning
- Effective assessment
- Formative and summative assessment
- A framework for planning, teaching and assessment
- Self-assessment
- Transition
- Asset languages and the languages ladder
- Monitoring.

## Assessment for learning – raising pupils' achievements

> Assessment for learning (AfL) is a powerful way of raising pupils' achievement. It is based on the principle that pupils will improve most if they understand the aim of their learning, where they are in relation to this aim and how they can achieve the aim (or close the gap in their knowledge.) It is not an add-on or a project; it is central to teaching and learning.
>
> (DCSF, 2008)

AfL should be precisely what it says. Children's learning should develop and progress through the teacher's assessment and the pupil's self-assessment.

Research has identified 10 principles of AfL:

1. It is part of effective planning.
2. It focuses on how students learn.
3. It is central to classroom practice.
4. It is a key professional skill.
5. It has an emotional impact.
6. It affects learner motivation.
7. It promotes commitment to learning goals and assessment criteria.
8. It helps learners know how to improve.
9. It encourages self-assessment.
10. It recognises all achievements.

> (Assessment Reform Group 2002)

The definition of each of these principles can be found on the website of the Assessment Reform Group at: www.assessment-reform-group.org/images/Principles%20for%20website.doc. The Assessment for Learning Strategy is available on the Department of Education website at: www.education.gov.uk/publications/standard/publicationdetail/page1/DCSF-00341-2008.

## Effective assessment

Using AfL in Primary Languages is the same as for any other subject. Teachers will use the assessment, self-assessment and planning cycle in order to further learning. They make judgements and evaluate constantly during lessons; this is the critical process to inform planning and to further learning. AfL has many facets: perhaps children's responses to questions, what questions they ask, how they are working with other children, what questions they ask each other. In all these interactions the teacher should be at the centre, interpreting and evaluating evidence. The whole time, the children should be aware of what they are learning and how they can improve.

An example is the teacher modelling a question and response and then asking the whole class a question that requires a whole-class response, e.g. 'Comment t'appelles-tu?' The teacher will notice who has responded 'Je m'appelle . . .' and who has not. The question will be asked again, and again observations will be made. When the same question is asked in groups, children's responses will again be monitored, and again when individual questions are asked. If the children are requested to put their hands up when they feel ready to answer, the teacher can assess who is confident and who is reticent, thus informing planning for the next session. Confident children will be ready to move on to the next stage of asking the question and answering; less confident children will need more practice in answering and in listening to how the question is phrased.

Feedback is also crucial because it needs to be given immediately so that children can self-assess and learn the value of errors in order to take responsibility for the learning process. An example of a child's self-assessment might be the pronunciation of the 'u' sound. The child pronounces it as 'ou' and recognises the difference when the correct pronunciation is demonstrated.

Child:   I need to practise 'u'. (*To teacher*) How will I do this?
Teacher:  Listen to the song 'Une poule sur le mur' and practise it at home. It shows the difference between 'u' and 'ou'.

The core principles for teaching and learning, developed from 'Excellence and Enjoyment' (DfES, 2003) are:

1.  Set high expectations and give every learner confidence they can succeed.
2.  Establish what learners already know and build on it.
3.  Structure and pace the learning experience to make it challenging and enjoyable.
4.  Inspire learning through a passion for the subject.
5.  Make individuals active partners in their learning.
6.  Develop learning skills and personal qualities.

(CILT Primary Languages website)

All these aspects interact with each other, and children will not progress as well as they could if all are not present. Point 4, 'Inspire learning through a passion for the subject', is the area that needs to be worked on in terms of Primary Languages! There are many teachers who are passionate about Primary Languages, but there are many who are not. These are the teachers who need as much support as possible in order to develop confidence and a 'can-do' approach. The Primary Languages co-ordinator is crucial in this and can help teachers to overcome their fears and reticence.

## Languages portfolio

Self-evaluation can be approached through the 'My Languages Portfolio' which is a Council of Europe initiative and was launched in 2001.

According to the CILT Primary Languages website, the portfolio is:

- a way to celebrate language learning and intercultural experiences
- an open-ended record of children's achievements in languages
- addressed to and the property of the learner
- a valuable source of information to aid transfer and transition.

It consists of three parts: a language biography, which takes the form of a diary where children can record their achievements and be aware of areas they need to develop; a dossier, which is a place to file work related to the biography, their Language Passport and other achievements; and a Language Passport, which is for children to record their cultural experiences, knowledge and experiences of other languages, and is an overview of the child's language knowledge.

There is a teachers' 'help' booklet to assist in using the Portfolio.

The European Languages Portfolio and the teachers' booklet can be downloaded at www.primarylanguages.org.uk/resources/assessment_and_recording/european_languages_portfolio.aspx. It is designed to accompany children throughout their KS2 schooling and provides an overview of children's achievements through self-evaluation; it is also helpful to keep samples of work with the portfolio

## Formative and summative assessment

Schools' assessment records should be manageable, otherwise they no longer serve their purpose. The class teacher's assessment record should also be manageable and should be regarded as a tool, a working document, and not simply as a means of providing evidence for Ofsted – although of course this is necessary. Records should tell teachers quickly what they need to know, and they should also be able to be completed speedily but accurately. All teachers need to develop assessment recording strategies that work for them, whether using highlighter pens or tick boxes. What they use doesn't matter, but what the format tells them does.

One school levels children's work at the end of each year using the National Curriculum levels and the Language Ladder descriptors. Record sheets are provided by the local authority adviser. Each class has one record sheet per year and each term is highlighted in a different colour. Completed sheets are passed on to the next class teacher. This is a manageable and effective way of carrying out assessment across the Key Stage. The assessment sheets are also used as a basis for writing end-of-year reports.

Assessment in Primary Languages is an area where many teachers feel that a formal approach will ruin children's enjoyment of the subject. It is true that most children thoroughly enjoy their language learning, and the thought of levelling and form-filling is off-putting. However, children are assessed formatively, constantly, in their phonics and literacy progress; it would not be a great leap to establish a formative assessment framework for Primary Languages. Teachers are well used to discerning children's progress in speaking, listening and comprehension. Jones and Coffey (2006) 'strongly assert that primary MFL learning should be located within a formative assessment framework that focuses on establishing what the children can do and offers feedback as to how they can progress. Progression in learning is a major issue of quality and enduring primary MFL provision' (p. 102). If children are not given feedback or assessed on their performance, they will not progress.

## A framework for planning, teaching and assessment

Figure 7.1 shows a possible model for a formative assessment framework for Primary Languages.

From this it can be seen that formative assessment and feedback are carried out during implementation, thus allowing the teacher to use errors for learning, and for children to understand that it is necessary and useful to make errors. Assessment and evaluation after

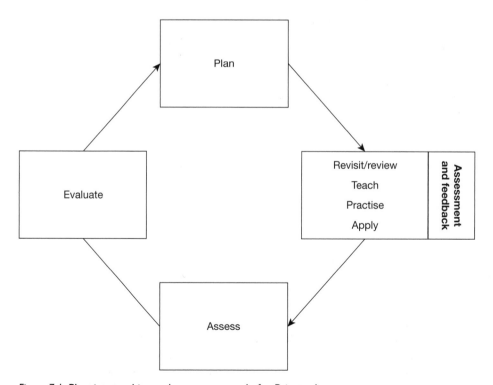

*Figure 7.1* Planning, teaching and assessment cycle for Primary Languages

the session feed into planning for the next session – particularly the 'revisit, review, practise and apply' component. It is a good idea for the format of the discrete session, as previously stated, to echo a discrete phonics session. This further deepens children's understanding of the links between literacy and Primary Languages.

### Primary Languages evidence and assessment checklist

A teachers' Primary Languages evidence check-list is helpful for assessment purposes.

* Observation notes (e.g. post-its) on the following:
    - motivation
    - attitude, enjoyment or otherwise
    - confidence
    - accuracy in pronunciation
    - responses to questions
    - asking questions in target language
    - working in groups/with partners
    - conversation notes with MFL co-ordinator, for example relating to assessment
    - transition and liaison with secondary
* Samples of work
    - any written evidence
    - ICT
    - photographic evidence
    - display
    - cross-curricular planning
* Audio samples
* DVD recordings of role play or activities
* Planning
* Resources (e.g. schemes of work, CDs, DVDs, ICT software, websites, books, photos, food and drink, puppets)
* Context (year group, EAL, teaching assistant support, native speaker, different class teacher [i.e. specialist language teacher], group work, whole class work, independent work, language(s) taught, partner schools).

## Self-assessment

Figure 7.2 is a sample page of self-assessment recording from a school in North Yorkshire.

The school is using objectives from the KS2 Framework for Languages and themes from the North Yorkshire Primary Languages scheme of work and converting these into 'I can statements'. The school has decided not to use the European Languages Portfolio and the class teacher has made an assessment booklet for each child in each year group in KS2. Children are invited to comment on their achievements and the teacher also makes comments and discusses targets with them. This is a pilot assessment scheme for the school, and it aims to level the children on the basis of their achievements in the following year.

| Year 4 Unit 7: Les Monstres | | | What I can do in French |
|---|---|---|---|
| **Learning objectives** | | | |
| I can speak clearly and confidently (O4.4) | | | • I can say some body parts |
| I can read aloud words I know (L4.3) | | | • I can read out loud at least 5 body parts and pronounce them accurately |
| I can listen for specific words or phrases and respond (04.2) | | | • I can follow instructions as part of a game or song |
| I can write simple words using a model (L4.4) | | | • I can write at least 5 body parts in the plural form |
| I can write phrases, using a model (L4.4) | | | • I can write short phrases or sentences to describe a monster |
| I can memorise a song and recite it (O4.1) | | | • I can sing Jean Petit from memory |
| Pupil comment | | | |
| Teacher comment | | | |

*Figure 7.2* Sample page of self-assessment recording from the North Yorkshire Scheme of Learning for Primary French

In addition to the 'prove it' column, it might be useful to include extra pages for the inclusion of assessment evidence based on the evidence checklist provided above.

AfL should not be confused with assessment *of* learning, which is summative and is used to measure pupils' achievements in the form of, for example, standardised tests. Testing for Primary Languages will be looked at in the section on transition in this chapter.

## Assessment for progression

The KS2 Framework for Languages is a tool for planning progression, and assessment can be made against the five strands. Examples of these are looked at in Chapter 3. The general principles underlying the framework are:

- An increase in the amount and complexity of language which the children can both use and understand.
- An increasing confidence in the children's use and understanding of language.

- A growing understanding of the children's own culture and those of others.
- An increase in the range and frequency of use of language learning strategies.
- Increased speed and fluency of response.
- Increased ability to reuse language in different contexts and topics.
- Growing confidence in dealing with unpredictable language.
- New insights into how language works.
- Increased confidence in deducing meaning using grammatical knowledge.
- Developing independence in language learning and use.

(CILT Primary Languages website)

Children should be able, then, by Year 6, to engage in simple conversations, write simple sentences and be aware of cultural aspects of the country of the target language (and of others) and have an insight into the working of the syntax of the target language and have deeper insight into the mother tongue's syntax.

Assessing children's progress against the criteria in the Framework for Languages can help to ensure that children reach the standard set out in the National Languages Strategy in 2002:

> By age 11 they should have the opportunity to reach a recognised level of competence on the Common European Framework and for that achievement to be recognised through a national scheme.

(DfES, 2002)

## Transition

Will Primary Languages learning help to facilitate language learning at secondary level? This is what is hoped and, further, that children will learn more languages at secondary level, helped by their understanding of 'how languages work', which they have developed at primary school.

However, for this to be possible, transition issues need to be considered. Transition is not just problematic for Primary Languages. As the research of Galton, Gray and Ruddock (1999) has demonstrated, schools have been more concerned with the social and administrative procedures of what they term 'transfer' than the pedagogic issues of transition.

Assessment plays a vital role in the successful transition of Primary Languages learning. The point about assessment is that it has to be referred to, considered and taken into account. It is a two-way process between teachers. Any transition assessment has to be carried out with this in mind. Liaison and consultation between teachers at primary and secondary level has to happen in order for secondary teachers to be aware (as far as possible) of children's capabilities and build on their learning, rather than repeat what the children have already covered.

There are many examples of good practice in this, but the key principles are:

- Primary and secondary schools working together:
    - exchange of documentation (records, portfolio, children's work);
    - mutual lesson observations;
    - co-teaching, preparing children for KS3 learning strategies whilst still in Year 6;

- celebrating Primary Languages achievements through events with Year 7 (perhaps a café, fashion show, concert);
- Year 7 children writing to Year 6 children in the target language, describing school and language lessons – peer contact and tutoring;
- passing planning and details of work covered to the secondary school so that Year 7 teachers are completely aware of work that has been covered and are aware of what and how to build on children's learning and how to adapt KS3 scheme of work.

- Collaboration works best when secondary teachers can embrace primary methodology in Year 7 and primary teachers can benefit from secondary teachers' expertise in languages.
- Sustained contact between primary and secondary school.

It is the sustained contact between KS2 and KS3 that is the most important, fostering and developing an awareness of issues that may arise and that can be addressed in order to facilitate the development of children's Primary Languages learning at both levels. It was this crucial element that was absent during the 1970s and that caused the pilot to fail. The fall-out from that pilot is still in evidence today.

## The Languages Ladder

The Languages Ladder is a national recognition scheme for languages that was pledged by the National Languages Strategy for England in 2002 and reflects the descriptors from the Common European Framework, the National Qualifications Framework and the National Curriculum. It recognises achievement in the four language skills and is made up of a series of 'I can' statements. It recognises a 'ladder' of achievement from beginners' level to mastery level (Figure 7.3).

| National Qualifications Framework | National Curriculum levels | General qualifications | Language Ladder stages | Common European Framework |
|---|---|---|---|---|
| Entry level | 1, 2, 3 | Entry 1, 2, 3 | Breakthrough: 1–3 | A1 |
| Level 1 | 4–6 | Foundation GCSE | Preliminary: 4–6 | A2 |
| Level 2 | 7–EP | Higher GCSE | Intermediate: 7–9 | B1 |
| Level 3 | | AS/A/AEA | Advanced: 10–12 | B2 |
| Level 4–6 | | BA Hons | Proficiency: 13–15 | C1 |
| Levels 7 and 8 | | Masters and doctorate | Mastery: 16 and 17 | C2 |

*Figure 7.3* Languages Ladder qualification levels

## Asset Languages

Asset Languages is a relatively new assessment scheme and the qualifications are based on the 'I can do' statements of the Languages Ladder. Each skill is assessed separately. According to the Asset Languages website:

> Asset Languages qualifications are recognised and transferable – they are worth something and can be compared on the national qualification framework to other awards.
>
> (Asset Languages)

## Monitoring

It is important for the co-ordinator or subject leader to monitor the teaching of Primary Languages on a planned basis. This gives important messages to staff that Primary Languages is an established element of the curriculum and is part of the whole-school ethos. Monitoring can be carried out in a variety of ways – classroom observation; collecting in children's work; observing displays; and discussion with staff and children. A good idea is to monitor on a two-yearly cycle. In this way progress can be measured within LKS2 and UKS2 and also across the transition from Lower to Upper. Any issues can then be identified and put into the school improvement or development plan.

Assessment and feedback is a two-way process between teacher and pupil, as is shown in Figure 7.4.

Primary Languages learners need to learn how to use and structure language rather than learning isolated lists of individual words. Learners need to move from knowing vocabulary

---

**Teacher**

Ensures Learners:

- Understand Learning objectives
- Are aware of success criteria
- Receive immediate (if possible) and effective feedback
- Are asked questions to promote learning
- Are given opportunities to ask questions to promote learning
- Correct errors

**Learners**

- Are engaged
- Understand how to self-assess
- Understand how to evaluate learning
- Understand how to improve learning
- Understand errors are necessary to improve learning

---

Figure 7.4 Exemplification of feedback, assessment and self-assessment – the two-way process between teacher and learner (adapted from Shirley Clarke, 2004)

to using it productively and manipulating words as necessary. Feedback is essential to ensure that the learner develops the skills and knowledge to generate language.

> When anyone is trying to learn, feedback about the effort has 3 elements: recognition of the desired goal, evidence about their present position and some understanding of a way to close the gap between the two.

(Black and Williams, 1998)

## Reflection

- Think about assessment methods you have observed or used – are they appropriate for assessing Primary Languages? How can they be adapted?
- What elements do you need to work on in order to develop your own assessment practice?
- What vocabulary do you need to develop for praising pupils and for giving oral feedback?

# Chapter 8

# Inclusive practice in Primary Languages

This chapter considers:

- children with special educational needs;
- how gifted and talented children can be identified in language learning;
- how languages work;
- EAL children and Primary Languages.

## Why do we need inclusion?

We need inclusion because children will have a part to play in society. An integrated schooling is good preparation for an integrated life. All children have an equal right to membership of the same groups as everyone else – it is a human rights issue!

Principles for inclusive practice in primary education are illustrated in the diagram in Figure 8.1.

With specific reference to Primary Languages, the model of learning objectives in Figure 8.2 can be used as follows:

- review and revisit prior learning
- maintain high expectations
- use the KS2 Framework for Languages to set objectives, starting from the year/age group-related objective but selecting earlier or later objectives as appropriate
- ensure that children have opportunities to speak in the target language
- use the target language where possible.

Overcoming potential barriers to learning (Figure 8.3) can be achieved by including the following approaches:

- using specialist equipment
- working with other adults/support
- using multi-sensory approaches
- management of behaviour.

| Teaching Styles | Learning Objectives | Access |
|---|---|---|
| Ensure different teaching styles are employed (VAK) and differentiation addressed | Learning objectives are appropriate | Ensure learning is accessible |
| ←————————————————— Inclusion —————————————————→ | | |

*Figure 8.1* Three principles for inclusion (adapted from the National Curriculum)

| Teaching Styles | Learning Objectives | Access |
|---|---|---|
| Ensure different teaching styles are employed (VAK) and differentiation addressed | Learning objectives are appropriate for all learners Differentiation takes account of G & T, SEN | Ensure learning is accessible |
| ←————————————————— Inclusion —————————————————→ | | |

*Figure 8.2* Inclusion in Primary Languages – learning objectives (adapted from the National Curriculum)

Teaching styles that are responsive to the children's needs require the teacher to:

- value everyone
- secure motivation and concentration
- assess pupils' needs and use this information to inform teaching
- set challenging/achievable targets.

An inclusive Primary Languages discrete session will therefore:

- review prior learning
- have clear learning objectives

| Teaching Styles | Learning Objectives | Access |
|---|---|---|
| Ensure different teaching styles are employed (VAK) | Learning objectives are appropriate | Ensure learning is accessible: EAL, SEN and disability considered Children are able to achieve ↓ |
| ← Inclusion → | | |

*Figure 8.3* Inclusion in Primary Languages – access (adapted from the National Curriculum)

- ensure that learning objectives and success criteria are shared with the pupils
- have variety – visual, auditory and kinaesthetic
- have pace
- have a high level of interactivity
- have many opportunities for talk and collaborative work
- use appropriate resources.

In addition to the above, for Primary Languages teaching the target language always needs to be practised and then applied. Learning should always be reviewed in a plenary.

Thus, an inclusive Primary Languages session is all about good teaching, using principles that the teacher is familiar and comfortable with. Two quotes from practising teachers are appropriate here:

> A lesson that doesn't include everyone is an incomplete lesson.
> In planning a lesson we imagine it from the children's point of view.

## Children with special educational needs

When I was teaching Primary Languages at the outset of my career, two class teachers informed me at the end of the first term of a Primary Languages project (which then continued for seven years!) that they had thought that the special educational needs (SEN) children in their classes would not be able to achieve what was expected of them during the sessions. However, they had been pleasantly surprised on several occasions by the extent of the children's achievements. These comments were obviously extremely interesting, and in discussions with the class teachers we speculated that, because I had not known that the children in question had any kind of learning difficulty, my expectations for them had been

| Teaching Styles | Learning Objectives | Access |
|---|---|---|
| Ensure different teaching styles are employed (VAK) to engage all learners; opportunities provided for all social, cultural and ethnic groups; assessment addressed; learning environment considered | Learning objectives are appropriate | Ensure learning is accessible |

Inclusion

*Figure 8.4* Inclusion in Primary Languages – teaching styles (adapted from the National Curriculum)

the same as for the rest of the class. We also speculated that perhaps their good performance and confidence might also have been related to the fact that none of the children in the class had any prior knowledge of French, and thus they were all at the same level of learning. The children did not, therefore, start out with any feelings of inferiority or anxiety, and so their confidence was increased. The children clearly enjoyed the lessons and made good progress.

Since that first project, over a period of 15 years I have taught Primary Languages continuously in several schools, in some as a peripatetic specialist and in others as a class teacher teaching the whole school Primary Languages. Throughout that time, my observations have concurred with those of the first project. SEN children generally perform well in Primary Languages, particularly over the first couple of years. I think that my colleagues' original speculative comments were true, but I feel that it is also related to the fact that the teaching emphasis was on speaking and listening, and not reading and writing. Clearly, a child who is struggling with recording and reading in English will also struggle with recording and reading in another language.

Other speculations and anecdotal evidence relate to the fact that many SEN children's speaking and listening skills were enhanced by Primary Languages sessions and their confidence levels during oral sessions remained high. Teachers observed that in the sessions following any Primary Languages input, concentration was improved.

Once reading and writing skills were introduced, extra visual support and other strategies were necessary to consolidate the learning of SEN children.

SEN children are likely to have poor memory skills, perhaps along with weak sound discrimination. Exposing children to more sounds in the new language can help with this, and activities such as listening to songs and asking for a physical response when they hear a particular sound are very beneficial.

During a European Day that I held in one school, an SEN child flourished during the can-can dance session; the teacher made it very acrobatic and the child was the star of the show. He also enjoyed the food aspect; we enjoyed European food on many occasions and this was an area that he engaged in fully. Primary Languages, like other subjects, should be multi-sensory and cater for different learners. In this way, motivation and interest can be sustained. This same child had a box of resources and activities that he could engage with when it was occasionally not possible for him to be included with the whole class. This consisted of different games and puzzles, amongst other things. Including Primary Languages activities such as songs, pictures and matching games in the box enabled him to still feel part of the Primary Languages learning in the class. More empirical research is needed in this area in order to develop understanding of the impact and benefits for SEN children of learning Primary Languages.

Other strategies that can be used to support SEN children are:

- mixed-ability talking partners;
- giving children who may be having difficulties as much practice as possible in role-play situations with higher ability children;
- clapping rhythms of words to help children memorise the number of syllables and to prompt their memory;
- using resources, such as counting apparatus in number sessions;
- also in number sessions, ensuring that children who may find it difficult to follow number games at speed are given numbers that they are secure with, so as to build confidence;
- using display; for example, pictures of instructions, which can be pointed to in order to clarify meaning;
- using more visual prompts;
- encouraging whole-class and group responses initially, so as to build confidence;
- giving children more thinking time when asking questions and ensuring that they feel ready to answer questions. A simple strategy is just to ask all of the class to put their hands up when they feel ready to answer any questions. This is also a useful formative assessment strategy;
- using personal electronic sound and word-bank files for children to practise with when they have any spare time;
- using IWB resources, which are often appealing for SEN children, particularly if the resources are properly interactive, and not passive;
- using song, a good motivator for children and an inclusive, enjoyable activity for all children. It is always helpful to include actions and activities with music to promote active learning;
- having alternative forms of recording available, e.g. voice recorders, scribing by a teaching assistant, drawing, colouring, word processing;
- showing different genders in different colours on the IWB or whiteboard to assist understanding.

As in all subject areas, children need to be aware of assessment criteria. Targets and questioning should be specific and discussion should be used during each session. If children are not guided when they make errors or have misconceptions, they will become afraid of attempting to participate. Developing a fear of making mistakes is one of the worst circumstances for any child learning a second language. It is vital for children to understand that progress is made through errors, and if they don't attempt to speak it is impossible to gauge understanding. Praise and encouragement are vital.

## How gifted and talented children in Primary Languages can be identified

A gifted and talented child in Primary Languages is likely to have excellent pronunciation, respond quickly to questions and have good recall and application of grammatical constructions used in sessions. He or she is also likely to want to communicate in the language.

If a child is gifted and talented in learning languages he or she is likely to be motivated to develop awareness and to show keenness to learn other languages besides the chosen school language. He or she will also be apt to demonstrate enthusiasm for finding out more about different cultures.

## How languages work

Primary Languages learning can be linked to Literacy by giving children opportunities to identify and compare grammatical features in different languages and by identifying text types. This approach is very beneficial for gifted and talented learners because it gives them an opportunity to 'dig deeper' and to discover the similarities and differences in languages and investigate how they 'work'. A problem-solving/investigative approach can be taken so as to deepen children's understanding.

Encourage children to identify and perhaps highlight key words and word classes, to look for cognates, to derive meaning and to consider punctuation. For example, looking at question marks could give children clues as to which words are interrogative. These activities will all assist in linking Primary Languages to literacy and reinforce comprehension not just of the Primary Languages syntax and grammatical structure but also that of the mother tongue. Texts can be embedded with any subject, as the examples in the following list show.

- **History**: An account of the Spanish Armada, the French Resistance or an Astérix text which could lead to interesting research on the Celts.
- **Art**: Children could look at the lives of different artists (the Impressionists offer rich resources); encourage research into Gaudí (look at the website in Spanish dedicated to the artist, where children can derive meaning: www.britannica.com/EBchecked/topic/226989/Antoni-Gaudi and then check the translation: www.greatbuildings.com/architects/Antonio_Gaudi.html).
- **RE**: Festivals offer many possibilities. For example, look at translations of the Bible in other languages (www.bibleserver.com/index.php?mode=text&trl_desig=BDS&language=fr&gw=go) as well as of other Holy books.

- **Geography**: Look at maps in the target language that include physical features, so that the children can develop vocabulary and also derive meaning. Look at Michelin guides in the target language, which again will help them to derive meaning. This activity could be linked with partner schools in order to demonstrate relevance and encourage motivation.
- **Websites for leisure interests** can be viewed in English, French, German, Spanish and Portuguese. For example, for football, the FIFA website: www.fifa.com/index. html?language=en. La Redoute is a shopping site that originated in France but is now international: www.laredoute.fr/. Many activities can be based around such sites, particularly in numeracy, but links such as those suggested also offer possibilities for literacy.

The possibilities for embedding Primary Languages texts are many and provide excellent opportunities for intercultural understanding and research.

Providing an appropriate curriculum for gifted and talented children will be challenging for the non-specialist teacher, for whom identifying such children in Primary Languages could be problematic for a number of reasons, such as non-familiarity with pronunciation or a lack of confidence in grammatical construction or in giving children more complex constructions in order for them to progress. This could well lead to some children under-achieving. It is important for teachers who lack confidence to liaise closely with Primary Languages co-ordinators and advanced skills teachers within the local authority in order to further their professional development and thus increase the opportunities for gifted and talented children in their classes.

## EAL children and Primary Languages

How do children with English as an additional language (EAL children) perform in Primary Languages? Research by Cummins (1984) and by Thomas and Collier (1997) indicates that it takes as long as seven years for pupils learning English as an additional language to acquire a level of English proficiency comparable to that of their native English-speaking peers. How, then, does this impact on their Primary Languages learning? The CILT Primary Languages website poses these questions in relation to EAL children and Primary Languages:

- What knowledge and skills do children who have English as an additional language bring to the primary languages classroom?
- How can we extend these skills?

The following might be a point for discussion:

An EAL child's progress will be hindered if he/she has to learn another language at the same time. He/she will become confused and both languages will suffer.

In considering this argument, it might be helpful to look at the questions posed above and to consider the advantages that the EAL children might have over their English-speaking peers:

- EAL children are proficient in one language and are already learning another. As such, they will be aware of language learning strategies and skills.
- They are attuned to listening for key words to derive meaning.
- They will know that they have to listen attentively in order to understand and progress.
- They understand that gesture and mime are important for understanding.
- They know that making errors is part of language learning.
- The Primary Languages common language will likely be new to all of the children, which places them on an equal footing with the other children.

EAL children are in a position to 'transfer their linguistic and cognitive skills from one language to another' (CILT). This all suggests that, rather than being at a disadvantage in learning Primary Languages, EAL children are actually advantaged and will put to good use all the skills they have acquired in their English language learning to enhance their Primary Languages learning.

EAL children will, however, be at different levels. Some might be at the basic interpersonal communicative skills (BICS) stage; others may have reached the cognitive academic linguistic proficiency (CALP) stage. Activities that children engage in at the BICS level will be less cognitively demanding, will be context embedded, and most likely based on repetition and imitation (Figure 8.5, quadrants i/iii). Children at the CALP level will be able to tackle activities that are cognitively demanding and less context embedded (Figure 8.5, quadrants ii/iv).

This can be exemplified in terms of activities as shown in Figure 8.6.

For primary teachers, additions to quadrant i might include greetings, conversations and role play. Quadrant ii might take into account daily routine interaction such as taking the register and classroom instructions.

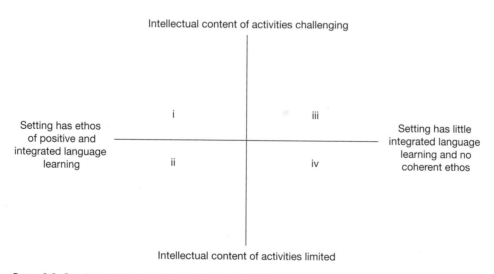

*Figure 8.5* Quadrant (1) adapted from Cummins (1984)

| Language Activities with Low Challenge Intellectually | |
|---|---|
| **Little Integrated LL and No Coherent Ethos** | **Positive Ethos of Integrated Language Learning** |
| Little time allocated, little progress made<br>Little opportunity given to speak<br>Lack of enthusiasm generated<br>Repetition not used creatively<br>Children unaware of what they are learning<br>Greetings but no gesture<br>Use of videos without follow-up | Children use language for specific purpose<br>and practise daily – e.g. asking to change<br>books, sharpen pencil etc<br>Songs with actions<br>Language learning relates to other areas<br>of the curriculum |
| **Challenging Activities – Developing Language Learning Skills** | |
| **Developing Specific Vocabulary and Skills** | **Developing Ability to Articulate Feelings and Response** |
| Art lesson which develops intercultural<br>understanding through learning about artist<br>and using vocabulary relating to technique<br>Numeracy lessons which use vocabulary to<br>apply concepts and calculation<br>Learning about festivals and beliefs in R.E. | Response to artwork and ability to<br>discuss response<br>Reflecting on errors and response<br>to and reflection on festivals<br>and beliefs |

*Figure 8.6* Quadrant (2) adapted from Cummins (1984)

It is also worth mentioning that EAL teaching strategies are very similar to Primary Languages strategies, such as:

- having a supportive environment and giving children an opportunity to experiment without fear of making mistakes;
- modelling the new language and planning opportunities to use it with peers and adults so as to develop confidence in speaking;
- using visual support such as props, artefacts, pictures, prompts and ICT;
- providing opportunities to practise spelling in the new language, which can help an EAL learner with spelling in English;
- using language creatively, for example, poetry, word play;
- providing support with literacy terminology/metalanguage;
- using first-language/English and language/English dictionaries;
- identifying borrowed words;
- collecting meanings and origins of proverbs;
- inventing word games and puzzles.

Thomas and Collier's thoughts on the influences on the EAL learner can be adapted as shown in Figure 8.7.

The influences on EAL learners that contribute to their Primary Languages learning are shown in Figure 8.8.

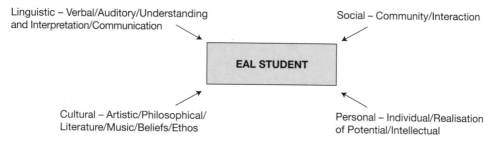

Figure 8.7 Socio-educational stimulation and impact on the EAL learner

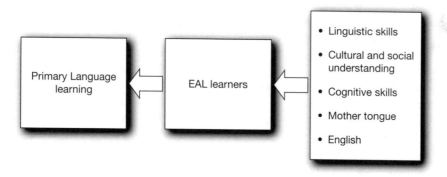

Figure 8.8 Influences on EAL learners that contribute to their Primary Languages learning

The CILT Primary Languages website states that: 'Anecdotal evidence from teachers suggests that EAL learners are often amongst the more able children in the primary language classroom, and bring to the classroom a wealth of experience and knowledge about language and language learning.'

Already having the skills in place to learn another language will surely support Primary Languages learning rather than hinder it. The primary teacher can use the already advanced linguistic skills of EAL learners to great advantage to ensure that Primary Languages learning is a positive experience not just for the EAL learner but for the whole class.

Lastly, Kenner (2000) suggests the following ideas to encourage young bilingual learners as writers by strengthening the dialogue between home and school:

• As part of whole-class discussions, invite bilingual children to talk about anything they have been reading or writing at home in any language. You can make it clear that you are interested in all sorts of activities: for example, have they watched cable or satellite TV in a home language? Have they got any DVDs or digital camera videos? Have they seen parents or grandparents reading a newspaper?

- Children may be shy about mentioning their home-language literacy activities until a multilingual literacy environment begins to be established in the classroom. Once they see their teacher working with texts in a number of languages, they will have evidence that bilingualism is part of school learning and they will feel comfortable about telling you what they know.

- Monolingual children will probably want to have something 'special' to talk about too. They are likely to add their own language and literacy experiences to the discussion (for example, when we worked with the *Lion King* audio-book in Spanish in the nursery, another child brought in her *Lion King* in English and we used both). This is a valuable way of finding out more about the home knowledge of all the children in the class.

- You could ask children whether anyone in their family writes in any language besides English. An open-ended question such as 'Can you show me how your grandmother writes?' or 'Would you like to do some writing in Chinese/Turkish . . .?' can stimulate children to engage in emergent writing. The presence in class of materials in their home language is a great support, particularly if the children themselves have brought in their favourite items (such as a photo album).

- The 'reading folder' which children take to and from school can be used for a two-way exchange of literacy items. As well as taking storybooks home from the classroom, children can be encouraged to bring in anything they have been reading at home. This will help teachers to find out about the immense variety of literacy activities the children enjoy. In our experience in the nursery, items which might appear in the folder can range from leaflets and cereal packets to Chinese storybooks, Indian film magazines and a birthday card from Thailand. The reading folder gives status to the materials carried in it and shows that home literacy is considered important in the classroom.

- A similar two-way exchange can be established with writing done at home and at school. If the teacher shows examples of children's emergent writing done in the classroom, parents will realise that emergent writing done at home is of interest to the school and be encouraged to bring in examples, either in a carrier bag or in the reading folder or similar 'writing folder'. Children will soon choose items they want to bring into school.

- Time spent on family literacy workshops will reap ample rewards. The workshops forge closer relationships between teachers and parents and provide informal opportunities to discuss children's learning. They are an excellent way of enabling parents and children to write together in school.

(NALDIC)

## Reflection

1.  Consider the following scenarios:

    - a newly arrived isolated EAL child
    - a pupil with behavioural difficulties
    - a Year 6 gifted and talented child.

Consider ways of including these pupils in:

- starter activity or game
- role play situation
- plenary.

2. What might be specific potential barriers to learning for Primary Languages?

# Chapter 9

# Developing competence and the future of Primary Languages

This chapter considers the future of Primary Languages within the primary curriculum, looking at the perspectives of trainee, teacher and provider. The following areas will be examined:

- Sustainability
- ICT in Primary Languages
- The role of the Primary Languages co-ordinator
- Practitioner research.

## Sustainability

How sustainable is primary languages in reality? The training and resources that have been developed have rendered the possibility of Primary Languages' (a) being accepted and (b) being deliverable much more likely. It is still fragile, however, and it is vital that potentially damaging issues continue to be addressed. The issues of sustainability can perhaps be summed up as follows:

1. Training
2. Schools' and teachers' confidence, commitment and attitude
3. Delivery models
4. Progression and transition.

At the time of writing, the government's stance on Primary Languages is not known other than it has made clear that it views language learning as 'part of the **essential knowledge and understanding** which all pupils should have to take their place as educated members of society' (Department for Education 2010).

In September 2010 a national survey of local authorities, across 100 local authorities (out of 152), by CILT revealed very positive attitudes towards Primary Languages amongst schools. All 100 local authority advisers stated that four out of five schools were teaching Primary Languages in curriculum time and 85 per cent of local authorities stated that Primary Languages should be made compulsory in the Primary Curriculum. However, some schools were beginning to retreat – particularly those where, perhaps, staff competence in Primary Languages was weaker. In addition, uncertainty as to funding clearly makes future planning far more difficult. The need for clear government direction as to the status of Primary Languages is paramount in order for it to be sustained. Many schools that have implemented the entitlement for Primary Languages have, however, recognised the enriching effect that language learning has across the whole curriculum. For example, children are enthusiastic to learn languages, intercultural understanding is enhanced, there are positive effects on speaking, listening and literacy attainment, and SEN children very often perform well in language learning. The momentum for the inclusion of Primary Languages as a statutory subject has been building since 2002 (and before), and for it to start to decline would be tragic and would entail another long, hard road towards ensuring that primary children have the same rights as other European children in language learning.

## Issues of sustainability

### Training

From the training perspective, there is a consistently growing and substantial amount of interest amongst both potential and actual trainees with regard to gaining competence and knowledge in the delivery of Primary Languages. Many initial teacher education (ITE) providers have made huge strides in ensuring that Primary Languages is integral to all programmes. This is vital in order to give trainees the important and positive message that Primary Languages is now part of the curriculum as an entitlement for children. Enthusiasm on the part of newly qualified teachers to teach languages is a key aspect of the sustainability of Primary Languages. Many ITE providers also have specialist Primary Languages programmes for both undergraduates and postgraduates. An important aspect of Primary Languages training is for providers to create opportunities within their programmes for trainees to have study and school experience abroad. Such experience demonstrates the value and relevance of language learning and inspires students to incorporate language learning into their practice. Enabling this experience to feed into their practice in schools is also crucial.

### WHAT OPPORTUNITIES EXIST FOR TRAINEES?

The TDA-funded four-week School Experience in Europe for undergraduates and postgraduates has been extremely successful and many trainees have participated in it. The benefits are summed up by the TDA as follows:

This training will:

- improve your job prospects: the *National Languages Strategy* will introduce an entitlement to language learning for every child in key stage 2 by 2010
- improve your foreign language skills, especially if you already have a good foundation
- give you greater awareness of another country's culture, enabling you to put the language into context and reflect this in your teaching
- provide you with a richer understanding of foreign schools and different teaching styles
- provide the host school with a unique opportunity to have a native speaker in their classroom for four weeks.

(TDA website, July 2010)

Trainees in my own institution cited their European experience as being the 'best thing they did at university' and returned fully convinced of the benefits of participating. It was challenging for them, but at the same time very rewarding. Most of them went not anticipating that they would achieve as much as they did, and were very surprised and gratified at what they accomplished. Teaching maths in English is hard enough, but teaching maths in French is doubly challenging. One trainee who struggled with conversation before he went and was very apprehensive about teaching in the target language went on to deliver an excellent maths lesson in French in the final week of his placement, having established a very good relationship with both the children and the class teacher. He was pleasantly surprised at his achievements, and on reflection, he realised that he had gained an enormous amount of knowledge during the four weeks and had begun to 'think in French', something he hadn't expected to be able to do. The experience should be designed to feed into the trainees' final training placement and make use of authentic resources that they have been able to develop both whilst on the placement and on their return. Trainees who wish to specialise in Primary Languages should, where possible, be placed in schools where Primary Languages is established and that have a wholehearted commitment to it.

## THE OVERSEAS MENTOR

The role of the mentor in school placements should be mentioned here. Mentors are necessary in all school placements, both overseas and in the UK.

When trainees are participating in overseas placements, the role of the mentor is an important one. Trainees will have to find their way around a new school in a foreign country, get to grips with a completely different education system and locate resources, the staff room, the lavatory and the photocopier, to name but a few things! Different institutions will have different approaches to appraisals and documentation, but it is crucial for the UK institution to meet with its counterparts overseas and visit the schools where the trainees will be teaching. Expectations regarding documentation can then be shared and planning can be discussed. Planning expectations are usually very different. The most important points are that the trainees should have an opportunity to reflect on their developing linguistic competence and to set realistic targets for the duration of their placements. The Common Reference Framework will assist the trainee and the mentor in target setting and ensure that the trainee is working towards any standards that are appropriate or outstanding from previous school placements in the UK.

Assessment of the placement is centred around the Common European Framework for Languages and the TDA Common Reference Framework, which is a bilateral agreement set up in 2005 to 'foster the reciprocal training of generalist primary class teachers for four weeks, as an integral element of the training programme in their home country'. It 'stresses personalised targets and formative assessment in a course structure agreed by English and French teacher trainers'. Comparative standards and targets are set with reference to the Qualified Teacher Status standards and the equivalent European Compétences. A model used by the University of Manchester encompasses the significant aspects of assessment that are likely to be of most benefit to the trainee (Figure 9.1).

The benefits are not just linguistic: gaining insight into another country's education system is interesting and useful for trainees, and they are able to observe, consider and evaluate teaching strategies, behaviour management and curriculum in the host country. Some trainees have returned for their placements inspired to engage in practitioner research.

*Figure 9.1* Assessment model for student placement overseas (University of Manchester)

Social benefits also emerge, as trainees return having coped with the demands not only of a challenging experience in school but also of living in another country. It is to be hoped that this invaluable opportunity will continue even though funding has been withdrawn.

### THE UK MENTOR

The mentor will sometimes be the Primary Languages co-ordinator, but this will not always be possible. It is important for mentors to have prompt sheets for appraisals from which to work, so that they can encourage trainees to appreciate the specific focus for a Primary Languages session. It is also important for mentors to receive appropriate training and to feel confident in assessing a Primary Languages session. An example of an appraisal prompt sheet that takes account of Primary Languages is shown in Figure 9.2.

There are areas within the appraisal prompt sheet that will be challenging for appraisers who do not have a background in Primary Languages – for example, pronunciation. Mentors will be as busy as everyone else and will be unlikely to be able to familiarise themselves with the content of a lesson before appraising it, and so it is key that the trainee have a healthy approach to self-evaluation, as well as a desire to improve.

| | Standards addressed |
|---|---|
| *Planning* | |
| • Is there a clear focus related to KS2 Framework for Languages/ Attainment Targets for Languages and/or QCDA schemes of work/scheme of work in use by school? | Q15, Q23, Q25b |
| • Is there specific mention of opportunities to use target language (i.e. scripted) for both trainee and pupil and is vocabulary specified? | |
| • For discrete sessions, is there clear structure and timing to the session (i.e. revisit/review; teach; practise; apply)? | |
| • If embedded session, are NC links/EYFS Framework (if appropriate)/Primary Framework strands referred to? | |
| • Does the trainee have clear understanding of either embedded or discrete approach? | |
| • Are there opportunities identified for consolidation throughout the week? | |
| *Teaching and learning* | |
| **Whole class (discrete session)** | Q14, Q25b |
| • Is previous work/prior learning reviewed adequately? | |
| • Does questioning offer opportunities for whole-class/group and individual responses? | |
| • Is pronunciation modelled effectively? | |
| • Are children given enough opportunity to speak? | |
| • Is adequate time allowed for children to formulate responses? | |
| • Are children given adequate opportunity for role play and to ask questions as well as answer? | |
| • Are sufficient praise words used in the target language? | |
| • Is there a clear focus to the aspect of work being addressed (e.g. Key Strands of KS2 Framework – oracy, literacy, intercultural understanding, knowledge about language, language learning strategies) | |
| • Are children encouraged to improve pronunciation through careful observation/practice? | |
| • Are instructions clear, and instructions vocabulary used appropriately? | |
| • Are children given the opportunity to demonstrate understanding through, for example, physical responses? | |
| • Are appropriate language learning strategies employed? | |
| **WHOLE class (embedded session)** | Q14, Q25a |
| • Are children aware of the purpose of the session? | |
| • Is the language content of the session at the cognitive level of the children in relation to the subject area being addressed, i.e. will the work allow the children to progress in both primary languages and the other subject(s)? | |
| • Are the children encouraged to use appropriate vocabulary? | |
| • Are there opportunities for the children to engage in purposeful talk, e.g. to develop ideas and rehearse their thoughts? | |
| • Are appropriate language learning strategies employed? | |

*Figure 9.2* Primary Languages lesson appraisal prompt sheet

| | |
|---|---|
| **Focus group (if appropriate)** | Q10, Q14, Q25a, Q25d |
| • Is there a clear focus to the group work? | |
| • Is there evidence of individual needs being met? | |
| • Does the trainee articulate the language correctly, asking/expecting the children to pronounce the words accurately themselves? | |
| • Are children encouraged to speak as often as possible? | |
| • Are children allowed adequate time to formulate responses? | |
| • Are appropriate language learning strategies employed? | |
| **Independent work (individual/paired/group)** | Q14, Q25a |
| • Is the work appropriate to the level of language knowledge of the children? | |
| • Are the children aware of how to approach words they may not understand using different strategies (e.g. cognates, dictionary use)? | |
| *Monitoring and assessment* | |
| • Did trainee use opportunities throughout the sessions for formative assessment? | Q26a, b |
| • What did the trainee find out about the children's learning at the point of teaching? (E.g., during group work, were the children able to apply their growing understanding or derive meaning from unknown words?) | |
| *Knowledge and understanding* | |
| • Does the trainee demonstrate secure subject knowledge, e.g. accurate syntax and grammatical understanding, accurate pronunciation, appropriate methodology, links between speaking and listening, reading and writing; links to other grammatical structures either in mother tongue or in other languages? | Q14, Q22, Q25c |
| • Does the trainee make accurate use of subject specific vocabulary and use the target language where appropriate? | Q25d |
| • Are the trainee's expectations of children's Primary Language knowledge skills appropriate and challenging? | Q1, Q26b |

*Figure 9.2 . . . continued*

Giving feedback to trainees and setting targets after any appraised session is clearly important. Discussions and feedback should take place as soon as possible after the lesson in order for the trainee to be able to reflect and consider how to improve. Targets should be set and mentors should make sure that any suggestions for improvement are acted upon in subsequent sessions.

Working with a Primary Languages cluster of schools can be very beneficial and rewarding. In one instance, some trainees on their final placements who had participated in the overseas placements worked together with their respective schools to provide a joint 'Languages Day' for all UKS2 children in the cluster. One school was used as the base and children from the other schools in the cluster travelled there and had an opportunity to work together on different activities throughout the day. The activities included Travel Agents, Story-telling and a café. Children had an opportunity not only to develop their linguistic competence but also to interact with children from other schools, which they found exciting and rewarding. Feedback from the day was very favourable on this point, and there were many comments along the lines of 'There should be many more days like this', and 'It would be great with other languages as well as French'.

One local authority has taken mentors to meet their counterparts in the European schools in which trainees spend their four-week placement. This has resulted in a highly motivated working group and is an example of very good practice in terms of liaison between teacher training providers, local authorities, schools and trainees.

Other possibilities for trainees to make overseas visits can be integrated into generalist and specialist programmes. It may be that some trainees are extremely interested in languages but wish to specialise in another area whilst at the same time wishing to develop their language competence. Opportunities for short trips (usually self-funded), such as a two-week visit as a teaching assistant, or perhaps in a setting where children learn outside of school (e.g. museum, residential centre) are options that are becoming popular. Such placements are of enormous benefit and offer trainees an opportunity to interact with native speakers and to further their intercultural understanding.

Giving students an opportunity to plan a residential visit for, say, Year 5 and Year 6 pupils has been a very popular option at my own institution. The trainees decide where in Europe they wish to visit and go on a reconnaissance trip, armed with a checklist of issues to consider when taking children on a trip abroad. The trainees then make a presentation of their findings, with an itinerary of a proposed trip, costings, health and safety considerations, travel, activities, assessment of children's developing linguistic competence, attitudes and motivation towards language learning and intercultural understanding, and all matters that they would need to take into account when taking children on such a trip.

Not all trainees are willing or able to participate in overseas placements, but, as all schools have to offer KS2 children the entitlement to learn a language, clearly all trainees have to be trained to deliver a Primary Languages curriculum! Given the future of languages at KS3/4, where all students will be encouraged to learn languages (and it may again become compulsory to take a language in KS4), it is likely that all future teacher trainees will have a knowledge of a language to GCSE level. This would clearly be an important addition to a primary teacher's skills base. However, at present trainees' language skills levels vary enormously, as do those of teachers.

In order to refine initial teacher training programmes so that all trainees are taken into account, the TDA has defined trainee entrants and the likely content of courses in the categories shown in Figures 9.3 to 9.7.

| Trainee entry profile | Content | Trainee coverage | Expectations during NQT year |
|---|---|---|---|
| • Trainee with language degree<br>• Postgraduate<br>• CEF C1/C2 | • Integrating language into curriculum<br>• Intercultural understanding<br>• Linguistic support<br>• KAL<br>• Primary pedagogy<br>• Subject leadership<br>• Transition KS2/3<br>• 4-week placement abroad | • Subject leadership in Primary Languages<br>• Lead on integration of language throughout school<br>• Teach LKS2 and UKS2 levels of KS2 Framework<br>• KS3 transition expertise | • Subject leaders who have an understanding of integrating language into the curriculum and across the school<br>• Deliver high-quality language lessons in own class |

*Figure 9.3* Platinum level – trainee with language degree

| Trainee entry profile | Content | Trainee coverage | Expectations during NQT year |
|---|---|---|---|
| • Trainee with language degree<br>• Postgraduate<br>• CEF C1/C2 | • Integrating language into curriculum<br>• Intercultural understanding<br>• Linguistic support<br>• KAL<br>• Primary pedagogy<br>• Subject leadership<br>• Transition KS2/3 | • Subject leadership in Primary Languages<br>• Lead on integration of language throughout school<br>• Teach LKS2 and UKS2 levels of KS2 Framework<br>• KS3 transition expertise | • Work towards being a subject leader who has understanding of integrating language into the curriculum and across the school<br>• Deliver high-quality language lessons in own class |

Figure 9.4 Gold level (non-mobility) – trainee with language degree

| Trainee entry profile | Content | Trainee coverage | Expectations during NQT year |
|---|---|---|---|
| • Trainee with language qualification below degree<br>• CEF B1/B2 | • Integrating language into curriculum<br>• Intercultural understanding<br>• Linguistic support<br>• KAL<br>• Primary pedagogy<br>• Subject leadership<br>• Transition KS2/3<br>• 4-week placement abroad | • Demonstrate integrating languages into the curriculum<br>• Teach LKS2 and UKS2 levels of KS2 Framework<br>• Support KS3 transition | • Deliver high-quality language lessons in own class<br>• Ability to integrate languages into the curriculum |

Figure 9.5 Silver level (mobility) – trainee without language degree

| Trainee entry profile | Content | Trainee coverage | Expectations during NQT year |
|---|---|---|---|
| • Trainee with language qualification below degree<br>• CEF B1/B2<br>• Undergraduate or postgraduate | • Integrating language into curriculum<br>• Intercultural understanding<br>• Linguistic support<br>• KAL<br>• Primary pedagogy<br>• Subject leadership<br>• Transition KS2/3 | • Demonstrate ability to integrate languages into the curriculum<br>• Teach lower levels of KS2 Framework | • Deliver high-quality language lessons in own class<br>• Work towards integrating languages into the curriculum |

Figure 9.6 Bronze (non-mobility) – trainee without language degree

| Trainee entry profile | Content | Trainee coverage | Expectations during NQT year |
|---|---|---|---|
| • Trainee with no language qualification<br>• Mono-linguistic English speakers<br>• Undergraduate or postgraduate | • Intercultural understanding<br>• Linguistic support<br>• KAL<br>• Primary pedagogy | • Teach intercultural understanding aspects of the KS2 Framework with language awareness, in collaboration with other language specialists | • Understand the role of languages in their classroom<br>• Deliver cultural aspects of the KS2 Framework and schemes of work<br>• Support the integration of languages across the curriculum<br>• Work towards delivering lower levels of KS2 Framework, with the support of other language specialists |

*Figure 9.7* Generalist (non-mobility) – trainee with no language qualifications

These models aim to take into account most entry profiles, although there might also be other sub-categories – for example, part-time postgraduate trainees who have a language degree but have not practised any kind of communication in that language for several years; or perhaps an undergraduate who has lived abroad and is fluent in a language but has no formal qualification in it. In such cases the trainee would obviously voice their preference as to the type of course content they wished to follow. The QCDA schemes of work are included in the original profiles, but it is likely, as previously mentioned, that the Primary Languages guidelines will still be followed by schools and institutions for some time.

The TDA has asked initial teacher education providers to develop courses that will reach not just trainees who have a degree of competence in languages, but also those who do not. In response to this, some institutions have developed upskilling as an integral part of their programmes and many have ensured that their modules cover Primary Languages pedagogy. Primary Languages conferences have proved a useful addition to many programmes, as well as ICT initiatives with partner Institutions in Europe.

The categories shown in Figures 9.3 to 9.7 allow providers to plan content and assessment appropriately. However, this is not without its challenges. Just as in schools, the teacher education programmes are crowded, and finding time for language provision is not easy. However, just as children will accept Primary Languages as part of their learning if it is presented to them as such, then so will trainees. Providers need to motivate trainees so that they will enter the profession not only confident in teaching Primary Languages but inspired to do so. Here, an important factor is that having a good grounding in languages helps trainees to 'stand out' in the jobs market. This has implications for teacher education, because modules need to be stimulating and relevant. Showing trainees that Primary Languages is relevant is often the crucial hurdle to be crossed, as it can be difficult to battle against disastrous language learning experiences and lack of interest. However, together with entitlement, the development of Primary Languages in teacher education programmes, inspection of Primary Languages provision in schools and teacher education, greater opportunities for teaching Primary Languages during school placements, opportunities for overseas travel and the explosion of resources for non-specialists – Primary Languages will, it is hoped, eventually be accepted in every school and training institution, just as is any other subject in the curriculum. Governments will change and policy will be redefined, but the aspirations of parents and many schools for a Primary Languages curriculum will not diminish.

## WHAT OPPORTUNITIES EXIST FOR TEACHERS?

For qualified teachers, the Primary Teachers' Project is one way to continue professional development. A partnership between the British Council and CILT, the project offers teachers an opportunity to receive 'a week of intensive language and methodology support, followed by a week of work shadowing in a primary school'. Funding is currently available through Comenius and the British Council.

Foreign language teaching assistants are also a valuable resource for schools. They bring opportunities for greater intercultural understanding and for the schools to interact with them in a foreign language. If teachers are unlikely to go abroad, then foreign language teaching assistants may represent the only opportunity that some staff have to engage with the target language. They can also help teachers who may be reticent about Primary Languages to see its relevance and potential.

Overseas trainees should also be an extremely welcome addition to schools' staff. Comenius Assistants, for example, are either qualified teachers or trainees who wish to improve their language skills. English teachers/trainees can work in any Comenius country (details are on the British Council website) and Comenius country trainees can also work in the UK. Placements are flexible, but can range from 13 weeks up to 45 weeks.

Comenius also encourages schools and teachers to work together in the following ways:

- in-service training (job shadowing, professional development courses)
- bilateral partnerships
- multilateral partnerships (involving at least 3 schools)
- local authorities across Europe working together
- Comenius multilateral partnerships for consortia, e.g. private companies, research centres, teacher training institutions, higher education institutions, local authorities, and schools (generally piloting materials).

The CILT has also developed an upskilling specification that is designed to be delivered within local authorities or perhaps in training within school clusters, and is thus locally managed. It is intended for teachers and teaching assistants with some degree of competence and, in its unmodified format, has high expectations of participants, but, as already mentioned, it is designed to be adapted by trainers for local delivery. Also, some teacher education providers and universities are offering the upskilling specification as an integral part of an MA programme in Primary Languages for teachers, and this will help considerably in upskilling the workforce generally.

## Schools' and teachers' confidence, commitment and attitude

The training for teachers needs to continue with local authority support, and schools need to ensure that they look to the advanced skills teachers, primary languages advisers and consultants for continuing professional development and to address issues that may arise within the school and that may threaten the progress of Primary Languages. As teachers' confidence increases, the integration of Primary Languages will become more stable and sure. However, as already mentioned, funding issues are preventing schools from planning adequately for the future. It remains to be seen whether the funding for Primary Languages remains in place, but it could become a factor that causes schools to retreat from developing and sustaining Primary Languages delivery.

Schools need to be aware of the opportunities detailed in the previous section to engage and inspire their teachers. It is only through teachers having such opportunities to develop their linguistic competence that those who may be reticent or indifferent will appreciate the value of learning a language. For this to happen, a whole-school ethos needs to be in place that demonstrates a whole-hearted commitment to Primary Languages. Whole-school policies and approaches need to be in evidence, and this should be a crucial aspect of any Ofsted inspection of Primary Languages.

In order for staff to appreciate and understand a school's commitment to Primary Languages the following should be in place/have been carried out:

- skills audit
- frank discussion between staff as to how Primary Languages should be implemented, i.e. which language, which model to use – specialist language teacher, class teacher delivery. This decision should be made after analysing the skills audit (see below)
- Primary Languages co-ordinator
- Primary Languages policy which takes into account:

    - rationale for teaching Primary Languages
    - aims of teaching Primary Languages
    - a clear programme/scheme of work identifying progression
    - curriculum planning/timetable planning
    - recording procedure
    - assessment procedures
    - reporting procedures
    - use of ICT
    - inclusion (SEN, gifted and talented, EAL, ethnicity, gender)
    - resources for all year groups
    - monitoring of all staff teaching Primary Languages.
    - training and professional development
    - plans to take Primary Languages teaching forward – e.g. overseas partnerships, Comenius projects, whole-school language events, trips abroad for specified year group.

Trainees placed in schools where this whole-school approach is not in evidence often comment on the negativity and indifferent attitude of some teachers and teaching assistants with regard to the teaching of Primary Languages. If children are on the receiving end of unenthusiastic delivery, the lack of interest communicates itself to them and affects their motivation and progression.

If the above suggestions are implemented it is likely that negative attitudes will change once it is seen how Primary Languages can enrich the curriculum.

## Delivery models

Schools determine which model of delivery is the most appropriate for them. Examples of delivery might be:

(a)   each class teacher
(b)   one internal specialist class teacher to KS2
(c)   external specialist teacher
(d)   native speaker not employed as a class teacher
(e)   secondary teacher from feeder school

If delivery is by any model other than a) or e) there are risks that Primary Languages provision could cease abruptly if the teachers leave, whereas if the school policy is for each class teacher to be responsible for Primary Languages teaching, it is far more likely to be sustained. Schools and teachers need to be encouraged to work towards the class-teacher model, in order for Primary Languages provision to be continued in the future.

## Progression

> While 'fun and games' are an important part of MFL and play a major role in motivating pupils, early learners also need to be challenged and to have their learning guided through clear stages of progression if initial motivation is to be maintained.
>
> (Jones and Coffey, 2006: 66)

Songs and games are an important part of the pedagogy for teaching Primary Languages. However, the above quotation is important to bear in mind so as to prevent the development of an attitude towards teaching languages such as 'doing a bit of French'. (Rather scarily, this phrase was used to me by an MP at an education meeting when I asked for his views as the introduction of Entitlement approached!) Progression within year groups as well as across year groups needs to be addressed.

Children should be able to:

- Build on prior learning
- Maintain motivation and engagement
- Demonstrate an increase in:

    - the amount and complexity of language which they can understand and use
    - the speed and fluency of response
    - confidence in deducing meaning using grammatical knowledge
    - confidence in understanding and use of language
    - ability to re-use language in different contexts and topics

- There should be a growth in:

    - understanding of children's own culture and those of others
    - the range and frequency of use of language learning strategies

     –   confidence in dealing with unpredictable language
     –   new insights into how language works
     –   developing independence in language learning and use across the range of skills

(CILT Primary Languages website)

These aspects should be assessed formatively and summatively.

Regular monitoring should take place, as with any other subject in the curriculum, to identify areas which need to be developed and also to celebrate areas that are successful.

Reporting procedures, too, should be in place, as for other subjects, as should be a clear approach to assessment (Chapter 7).

### Transition

Transition is the aspect of sustainability that gets most people hot under the collar and is seen as possibly the 'fly in the ointment'. This undoubtedly harks back to the Burstall report and its negativity regarding children's progress at secondary level after having received primary language teaching and in face of secondary teachers' lack of recognition of children's achievements in languages. Transition issues are looked at in depth in Chapter 7, so suffice it to say here that transition in Primary Languages needs to engender in children the following:

- an enthusiasm for learning
- confidence in themselves as learners
- a sense of purpose and achievement
- a sense of progression in responsibility and autonomy that matches their increase in age and social maturity.

(Galton, Gray and Ruddock, 2003)

Central to this is celebrating, building on and recognising children's achievements at primary level.

## ICT in Primary Languages learning

ICT can enhance children's learning in Primary Languages, just as it can in any subject area. However, it is necessary to emphasise that the role of the teacher is paramount and any ICT teaching that is used should be carefully considered. Can ICT do or deliver something better than the teacher? If not, then it is best not to use it. Primary Languages should be as interpersonal as possible, and the danger of some ICT or e-learning methods is that children become distracted by images and sounds and do not retain the objective of the session. However, ICT can greatly enhance interaction if it is used properly. There are many ICT techniques that work well, e.g. podcasting, flip videos and multimedia recording, which enable children (and teachers) to evaluate their own speaking and pronunciation and promote speaking and listening generally. The video camera provides opportunities for role play and animation.

IWBs enable the use of wonderful images and DVD clips to support language learning, especially in intercultural understanding, and there are many excellent programmes for teachers to use. IWBs also offer many opportunities for interaction, e.g. drag and drop, spotlight, hide, reveal, erase. These are all great additions to the primary teacher's portfolio of resources.

Video-conferencing and e-mail also open up possibilities for children to interact with their partner schools, for example, and provide opportunities for communicating in the target language. For more on this, see Chapter 6.

Video-conferencing can also be a means for schools in rural areas to have access to language learning if, for example, another school has more expertise or perhaps the only expertise in the area. One pilot project used a language specialist to teach a cluster of four schools via video-conferencing on a regular basis. These schools would otherwise have received little or no language teaching. The children were given tasks via interactive notepads and through speaking and listening. Whole-class teaching and group teaching were carried out, and teachers were present so that they could improve their own language competence and develop confidence to consolidate and embed language learning during the week. The pilot culminated in a group of children from each of the four schools making a trip to France, which inspired the schools to continue language teaching on their own. They developed links with partner schools and made further trips to visit them.

PowerPoint presentations with video clips and songs can also be used in video-conferencing.

Devon County Council has produced a publication entitled *Video Conferencing in the Classroom* (2004) which has many ideas and advice about the use of video conferencing. The CILT Primary Languages website has a wealth of information and advice about ICT resources in the KS2 classroom. See www.languages-ict.org.uk/.

## The role of the Primary Languages co-ordinator

The Primary Languages co-ordinator's role encompasses the usual aspects of such a role – that is:

* writing the school's Primary Languages policy and gathering evidence for Ofsted
* responsibility for managing resources and any budget for Primary Languages
* monitoring and assessment
* CPD and training
* supporting and advising staff
* assisting staff with planning.

In addition, the Primary Languages co-ordinator will most likely decide with the school's management team which language or languages the school should teach and how it should be delivered. This will depend on the skills base within the school and/or availability of specialist staff and, perhaps, native speakers.

Other areas of responsibility and aspects of the role might include:

* assessing training needs for staff: those of the Primary Languages co-coordinator as well as everyone else. This may entail a questionnaire and discussions to ascertain skill levels;
* promoting a positive ethos in relation to Primary Languages: commitment and patience are required for this, as there may be some teachers who are uneasy or uncomfortable with teaching Primary Languages;

- developing the international dimension within the school: the Primary Languages co-ordinator very often takes on this responsibility. This will entail developing links with schools overseas and also, perhaps, an education business partnership;
- understanding that there may not be other support within the school, in which case strong communication with local authorities and advanced skills teachers is vital;
- co-ordinating overseas trips for pupils (this is considered in depth in Chapter 6);
- liaising with parents;
- modelling sessions for staff;
- attending meetings of, and perhaps initiating, MFL cluster groups;
- liaising with secondary schools for smooth transition;
- co-ordinating Primary Languages events such as European or language days;
- encouraging performance of Primary Languages within the school, e.g. assemblies;
- reporting on the school's and children's progress in Primary Languages to the governing body and parents.

The Primary Languages co-ordinator will monitor the school's achievements, evaluate progress and identify areas for improvement, as with any other subject area. The appraisal pro-forma in Figure 9.2 is a good starting point for evaluation but it is not exhaustive, and schools and Primary Languages co-ordinators should adapt such documentation to suit their individual needs.

It may be that there is no obvious person to lead Primary Languages in a school. In such cases, the person who is nominated will need to rely heavily on local authority and advanced skills teacher support, and to devise a skills audit for the staff so as to identify which is the most appropriate language to teach. Training is paramount, and should be undertaken regularly. Courses are run by the CILT and local support groups around the country – there are 80 in all. Further information about the support groups and the services they offer can be found at: www.primarylanguages.org.uk/professional_development/local_support_groups.aspx.

In addition, CILT offers advice and networking opportunities.

## Practitioner research

As previously mentioned, trainees have returned from European placements inspired to research further into Primary Languages, and this should be encouraged, whether it be joint working with academics or research by qualified teachers for a Master's degree. Empirical research in many areas of Primary Languages is urgently needed to demonstrate the impact on learning for primary children. The research areas include SEN, ICT, training, links to literacy and phonics, cross-curricular approaches, EAL and Primary Languages, learning Primary Languages at the Foundation Stage/KS1, the use of the target language and transition.

The exciting progress made over the past twenty years needs to be built on with hard evidence to show the positive and rewarding benefits of language learning at primary level.

## Reflection

- Have you noticed any aspects of Primary Languages teaching in your placements/school that you feel warrant research?

- Consider whether you would be willing to travel to another country to develop your linguistic competence. If your immediate reaction is negative, think carefully why this might be.
- Do you feel that you have a good understanding of what progression in Primary Languages looks like?

# References and further reading

## Chapter I

Birdsong, D. (ed.) (1999) *Second Language Acquisition and the Critical Period Hypothesis*, Mahwah, NJ: Lawrence Erlbaum Associates.

Bruner, J.S. (1966) *Towards a Theory of Instruction*, Cambridge, MA: Harvard University Press.

Burstall, C., Jamieson, M., Cohen, S. and Hargreaves, M. (1974) *Primary French in the Balance*, Windsor: National Foundation for Educational Research.

CILT (2010) 'Primary Languages Survey', www.primarylanguages.org.uk/home/news/news_articles/primary_languages_survey.aspx.

CILT (n.d.) *Primary Languages*, www.primarylanguages.org.uk/home.aspx.

DfES (2002) *Languages for All: Languages for Life*, London: DfES.

European Commission (2008) 'Multilingualism: Language Learning', http://ec.europa.eu/education/languages/language-learning/index_en.htm.

Higher Education and Funding Council for England (2008) 'Graduates and Their Early Careers', www.hefce.ac.uk/pubs/hefce/2008/08_39/.

Krashen, S. (1981) *Second Language Acquisition and Second Language Learning*, Oxford: Pergamon Press.

Lenneberg, E.H. (1967) *Biological Foundations of Language*, New York: Wiley.

Nuffield Foundation (2000) *Languages: the Next Generation*, London: The Nuffield Foundation.

Ofsted (2011) 'Modern Languages Achievement and Challenge 2007–2010', www.ofsted.gov.uk/Ofsted-home/Publications-and-research/Browse-all-by/Documents-by-type/Thematic-reports/Modern-languages-achievement-and-challenge-2007–2010.

Open University, Christ Church University Canterbury and University of Southampton (2010) *Language Learning at KS2: Final Report*, London: CILT.

Worton, M. (2009) *Review of Modern Foreign Languages Provision in Higher Education in England*, London: HEFCE.

## Chapter 2

Bloom, B. S. (ed.) (1956)*Taxonomy of Educational Objectives, the Classification of Educational Goals – Handbook I: Cognitive Domain*, New York: McKay.

CILT, www.primarylanguages.org.uk.

CILT, 'QCDA Schemes of Work for Key Stage 2 Languages', www.primarylanguages.org.uk/resources/schemes_of_work/qcda_schemes_of_work.aspx.

DCSF (2005) *KS2 Framework for Languages*, London: DCSF.

Johnstone, R. (1994) *Teaching Modern Languages at Primary School: Approaches and Implications*, Edinburgh: Scottish Council for Research in Education.

Nuffield Foundation (2000) *Languages: the Next Generation*, London: The Nuffield Foundation.

Satchwell, P. and da Silva, J. (2007) *Speak Up! Getting Talking in the Languages Classroom*, CILT Young Pathfinder.

Sharpe, K. (2001) *Modern Foreign Languages in the Primary School: the What, Why and How of Early MFL Teaching*, London: Kogan Page.


## Chapter 3

Chomsky, N. (1957) *Syntactic Structures*, The Hague: Mouton (repr. Berlin and New York, 1985).

Chomsky, N. (1965) *Aspects of the Theory of Syntax*, Cambridge, MA: MIT Press.

DCSF (2004) 'KS3 National Strategy 2004–05', www.nationalstrategies.standards.dcsf. gov.uk/node/97274.

Department for Education (2009) 'Developing Language in the Primary School: Literacy and Primary Languages', http://nationalstrategies.standards.dcsf.gov.uk/node/188107.

Department for Education, 'Key Stage 3 Framework for Languages', http://national strategies.standards.dcsf.gov.uk/node/169162.

Department for Education, 'Primary Literacy Framework', http://nationalstrategies. standards.dcsf.gov.uk/primary/primaryframework/literacyframework.

Ofsted (2011) 'Modern Languages Achievement and Challenge 2007–2010', www. ofsted.gov.uk/Ofsted-home/Publications-and-research/Browse-all-by/Documents-by-type/Thematic-reports/Modern-languages-achievement-and-challenge-2007–2010.

Oxford, R.L. (1990) *Language Learning Strategies: What Every Teacher Should Know*, Wadsworth Publishing Co., Inc.

Rubin, J. (1975) 'What the Good Language Learner Can Teach Us', *TESOL Quarterly*, 9, 41–51.

Stern, H.H. (1975) 'What Can We Learn from the Good Language Learner?', *Canadian Modern Language Review*, 34, 304–18.

Weinstein, C. E. and Mayer, R. E. (1986) 'The Teaching of Learning Strategies', in M. Wittrock (ed.) *Handbook of Research on Teaching*, New York: Macmillan, pp. 315–27.


## Chapter 4

DfES (2003) 'Excellence and Enjoyment: A Strategy for Primary Schools', www. education.gov.uk/publications/standard/publicationdetail/page1/DfES%200377%20 2003.

DfES (2004) 'Primary Framework for Literary and Mathematics 2006', Primary National Strategy 20211–2006BOK-EN.

Devon Learning and Development Partnership (2007) *Take 10 (en français)*, Exeter: Devon Learning and Development Partnership.

Hamayan, E. (1986) 'The Need for Foreign Language Competence in the United States', in M. Sutton and D. Hutton (eds), *Concepts and Trends in Global Education*, Bloomington, IN: ERIC Clearinghouse for Social Studies/Social Science Education.

Jones, J. and Coffey, S. (2006) *Modern Foreign Languages 5–11: A Guide for Teachers*, London: David Fulton Publishers.


## Chapter 5

Blatchford, P., Russell, A., Bassett, P., Brown, P. and Martin, C. (2004) *The Role and Effects of Teaching Assistants in English Primary Schools (Years 4 to 6)*, London: DfES.

Cummins, J. (1981) 'The Role of Primary Language Development in Promoting Educational Success for Language Minority Students', in California State Department of Education (ed.), *Schooling and Language Minority Students: A Theoretical Framework*, Los Angeles: Evaluation, Dissemination and Assessment Center, California State University.

Cummins, J. (2000) *Language, Power and Pedagogy: Bilingual Children in the Crossfire*, Clevedon: Multilingual Matters.

Collier, V.P. and Thomas, W.P. (1989) 'How Quickly Can Immigrants Become Proficient in School English?', *Journal of Educational Issues of Language Minority Students*, 5, 26–38.

Webster, R., Russell, A., Blatchford, P. (2009) 'A Help or a Hindrance?' *Every Child Journal*, 1(2): 64–7.

## Chapter 6

Bhatt, A. Bhojani, N., Creese, A. and Martin, P. (2004) *Complementary and Mainstream Schooling: A Case for Reciprocity?* NALDIC Occasional Paper 18.

Blackledge, A. (1998) *Unit 4: Literacy and Bilingual Learners; Introduction to Bilingualism in Education*, Birmingham: University of Birmingham Educational Materials.

Byram, M. and Doyé, P. (1999) 'Intercultural Competence and Foreign Language Learning in the Primary School', in P. Driscoll and D. Frost, *The Teaching of Modern Languages in the Primary School*, London: Routledge.

Chomsky, N. (1965) *Aspects of the Theory of Syntax*. MIT Press.

CILT, 'Intercultural Understanding', www.primarylanguages.org.uk/resources/online_resources/intercultural_understanding.aspx.

Jones, J. and Coffey, S. (2006) *Modern Foreign Languages 5–11: A Guide for Teachers*. London: David Fulton Publishers Ltd.

Meyer, M. (1991) 'Developing Transcultural Competence: Case Studies of Advance Foreign Language Learners', in D. Buttjes and M. Byram (eds), *Mediating Languages and Cultures: Towards an Intercultural Theory of Foreign Language Education*, Clevedon: Multilingual Matters, pp. 136–58.

National Association for Language Development in the Curriculum, www.naldic.org.uk/.

Vistawide, 'World Languages and Culture', www.vistawide.com/languages/why_languages.htm.

## Chapter 7

Assessment Reform Group (2002) *Research-based Principles to Guide Classroom Practice*, London: Nuffield Foundation.

Asset Languages, www.assetlanguages.org.uk/.

Bevis, R. and Gregory, A. (2005) *Mind the Gap!* (Young Pathfinder 13), London: CILT.

Black, P. and Williams, D. (1998) *Inside the Black Box: Raising Standards through Classroom Assessment*, London: King's College.

DCSF (2008) 'The Assessment for Learning Strategy', Department for Education Archive, DCSF 00341–2008, https://www.education.gov.uk/publications/standard/publicationdetail/page1/DCSF-00341–2008.

DfES (2002) *Languages for All: Languages for Life*, London: DfES.

DfES (2003) 'Excellence and Enjoyment: A Strategy for Primary Schools', www.education.gov.uk/publications/standard/publicationdetail/page1/DfES%200377%202003.

Driscoll, P. (1999) *The Teaching of Modern Foreign Languages in the Primary School*, London: RoutledgeFalmer.

Galton, M., Gray, J. and Ruddock, J. (1999) *The Impact of School Transitions and Transfers on Pupil Progress and Attainment*, London: DfES Publications.

Jones, J. and Coffey, S. (2006) *Modern Foregin Languages 5–11: A Guide for Teachers*. London: David Fulton Publishers Ltd.

## Chapter 8

Buttaro, L. (2009) 'Language, Learning, and the Achievement Gap: The Influence of Classroom Practices and Conversation on Performance', PhD dissertation, Adelphi University.

Cline, T., de Abreu, G., Fihosy, C., Gray, H., Lambert, H. and Neale, J. (2002) *Minority Ethnic Pupils in Mainly White Schools*, Norwich: DfES.

Collier, V.P. (1995) 'Acquiring a Second Language for School', *Directions in Language and Education*, 1(4), www.thomasandcollier.com/Downloads/1995_Acquiring-a-Second-Language-for-School_DLE4.pdf.

Cummins, J. (1984) *Bilingualism and Special Education: Issues in Assessment and Pedagogy*, Clevedon: Multilingual Matters.

Gibbons, P. (1991) *Learning to Learn in a Second Language*, Newtown: Primary English Teaching Association.

Herefordshire Grid for Learning, 'Lessons for Gifted Linguists', www.thegrid.org.uk/learning/mfl/inclusion/ks3.shtml.

Kenner, C. (2000) *Home Pages: Literacy Links for Bilingual Children*, Stoke-on-Trent: Trentham Books.

National Association for Language Development in the Curriculum, 'Gifted and Talented', www.naldic.org.uk/ITTSEAL2/teaching/GAT.cfm.

Thomas, W. and Collier, V. (1997) *School Effectiveness for Language Minority Students*, Washington, DC: National Clearinghouse for Bilingual Education.

## Chapter 9

Bolster, A., Balandier-Brown, C. and Rea-Dickins, P. (2004) 'Young Learners of Modern Foreign Languages and Their Transition to the Secondary Phase: A Lost Opportunity?', *Language Learning Journal*, 30, 35–41.

CILT (2010) 'Primary Languages Survey', www.primarylanguages.org.uk/home/news/news_articles/primary_languages_survey.aspx.

Comfort, T. and Tierney, D. (2007) *We Have the Technology*, CILT.

Department for Education (2010) *The Importance of Teaching*, White Paper, London: Department for Education.

Galton, M., Gray, J. and Ruddock, J. (1999) 'Learning Bridges to Transition: The Impact of School Transitions and Transfers on Pupil Progress and Attainment', Homerton College, Cambridge DCSF Research Report No. 131.

Hawkins, E. (1999) '30 Years of Language Teaching', chapter 13 in *The Early Teaching of Modern Languages – A Pilot Scheme*, CILT.

Jones, J. and Coffey, S. (2006) *Modern Foregin Languages 5–11: A Guide for Teachers*. London: David Fulton Publishers Ltd.

Sharpe, K. (2001) *Foreign Languages in the Primary School*, London: RoutledgeFalmer.

TDA website (2010): www.tda.gov.uk.

# Index